WILD?
THESE CATS
ARE FURIOUS!

What's it like to have furries at the
bottom of your garden?

Heather Cook

Photographs by Roger Cook

Matador
9 Priory Business Park,
Wistow Road, Kibworth Beauchamp,
Leicestershire. LE8 0RX
Tel: 0116 279 2299
Email: books@troubador.co.uk
Web: www.troubador.co.uk/matador
Twitter: @matadorbooks

ISBN 978 1788035 842

British Library Cataloguing in Publication Data.
A catalogue record for this book is available from the British Library.

Printed and bound in the UK by TJ International, Padstow, Cornwall
Typeset in 11pt Aldine401 BT by Troubador Publishing Ltd, Leicester, UK

Matador is an imprint of Troubador Publishing Ltd

This book is dedicated to the memory of our much-loved boy,
Benjamin Wobble

Benjamin made wobbliness seem wonderful

ALSO BY HEATHER COOK

INTRODUCTION

One of my great delights as a child was visiting London Zoo, where I would watch the cats in the Lion House pacing up and down and savour every captivating thing about them – their beauty, movement and above all their smell. It was this exciting animal smell above all things that stayed with me. I was not repulsed by it, just aware that this was pure essence of primeval wildness.

As a very young child I was pre-occupied with animals being safe and I don't remember being disturbed initially by the sight of these magnificent creatures displaying what I came to realise was alarming evidence of distress with their obsessive pacing. However, as I became more aware of the world around me and read voraciously everything about animals that I could get my podgy little hands on, I realised that these beautiful cats were paying far too high a price for being 'safe'. By the time I reached my teens, the Zoo was the last place I wanted to visit.

When I was a small child in London, circuses seemed a thrilling and exotic spectacle. The public would be allowed to wander round outside the huge marquee viewing the performing lions, tigers, elephants, llamas and other unfortunate creatures in their cramped cages, but almost overnight what had seemed a treat became an acutely distressing experience for me. My poor parents must have been puzzled and hurt by the behaviour of this ungrateful child – a child who had on the circus' previous visit clamoured to be taken round to see the animals, but who now refused to go anywhere near the circus, accusing her friends of cruelty and callousness if they so much as looked at a poster. It was even worse than that: I bullied half the school into joining the Jack London League which opposed the cruelty inflicted on circus animals in the course of their training.

My mother must have put a lot of energy into calming enraged parents, who – I heard many years later – accused her of having a really scary daughter!

A few years later, I stumbled across the wonderful books by Mike Tomkies and fell in love with the Scottish Wildcat. In particular, I was fascinated by the story of Sylvesturr – a male wildcat who had been in London Zoo for 10 years and was transported by Mike to the Highlands to be released into the wild.

This magnificent creature had existed for all that time in a cage without having a thought in his great tomcat head about modifying his behaviour in the slightest. He had hated the human race from the moment of capture with an intensity that 10 years of incarceration had entirely failed to diminish. Against the odds, he not only survived when the pine-scented road to freedom finally opened up before him, but found himself a mate and fathered kittens.

A few more years passed and I found myself involved in cat rescue in the wilderness that is downtown Woking and although it was a world away from the Scottish Highlands, I certainly encountered some unexpected challenges. I should mention that my involvement did not come about as a result of a positive choice, but I would not have missed it for the world. In this book I recount some of the adventures I had with the distant cousins of Sylvesturr – cousins who I think he would have been proud to call 'family'.

Heather Cook

CHAPTER ONE

Baptism by Fur

Please bear with me when I say that things were different when I first plunged into the heady world of cat rescue. The Headquarters of Cats Protection in those days consisted of a couple of rooms in Slough and although everybody was terribly kind and supportive, there was precious little guidance available for well-meaning amateurs wanting to start up a new local group. Amazing though it now seems, there were no home computers and communications were on the hit and miss side of dodgy.

You could be forgiven for imagining that the group of people embarking on this project had some previous experience of animal work; well, actually we didn't. We had our own pet cats and we loved them, but apart from this the skills and experience we had amassed as civil servants, shop workers, air traffic controllers, teachers, bookkeepers and young mums hardly equipped us to face the challenges ahead. The saving grace, of course, was that we had no idea what those challenges would be.

It always amuses me when people make remarks like, 'She really seemed to think that love would conquer all! Can you believe the naivete of it?'. It amuses me because so often in my experience, love is the very thing that gets you through and keeps you going when any sensible person would have given up. This was certainly the case with Woking Group of Cats Protection League in those early days. The organisation

1 🐾

subsequently dropped 'League' from its title because it was deemed to be rather old fashioned, but they certainly didn't come any more old fashioned than us, so it suited us rather well.

If I gave any thought to what we might be in for during my daily commute to Waterloo, I suppose I imagined that we would be fostering and finding homes for strays and unwanted cats and kittens and that they would all be sweet, grateful creatures who would purr when spoken to and keep their claws firmly retracted at all times. Kittens might hiss in a rather endearing fashion, but we could probably cope with that.

I don't remember it ever crossing my mind that some of the cats we would be expected to help with might be quite rude. Actually, some of the people were rather rude as well, but we won't dwell on that here. I had heard about large colonies of stray cats being fed in hospital grounds and on various holidays abroad had been distressed to see the large numbers of hungry and homeless cats skulking outside hotels and apartment blocks, but this was Woking, for heaven's sake!

Our first brush with the wilder side of cat rescue came when we were asked if we could help with feeding a colony of feral cats in the local hospital grounds. This was a well-established colony and the cats were popular with staff and patients. The hospital in question was a large psychiatric institution and many of the patients had lived there for years. Although the hard-pressed nursing staff had cared about the cats by providing shelters and food, little had been done to limit their numbers – as we realised with something akin to panic when we first ventured into the grounds.

Our first visit was in daylight and only the boldest cats were in evidence, eyeing us suspiciously from a veritable shanty town of modified rabbit hutches and pallets. The second visit was at night and there were more cats and kittens than anybody could shake a stick at, even if they had felt so inclined. We tried to maintain an air of calm competence, but only a total idiot could have felt truly complacent. Somebody needed to do something and we had an uncomfortable feeling that the 'somebody' might be us.

We soon cobbled together a rota to help out with feeding and everybody involved was surprised at how quickly the different cat personalities emerged, even though it was obvious that these cats harboured some pretty negative feelings about us. There were the slinkers – slim shadows that slipped between the bushes and buildings to snatch a mouthful of food and retreat hastily into darkness; then there were the guardians – battered tomcats or ageing matriarchs that had seen life in the raw and weren't very bothered about anything as long as the food kept appearing. And, of course, there were kittens – not as many as there might have been because various people had done their best over the years to grab them when they were still tiny and find them homes, but enough to suggest that action over and above shoving down a few plates of food might be called for – and soon.

Feeding the cats called for nerves of steel; not because the cats showed any inclination to tear us limb from limb, but because some of the shadows emerging into the fitful torchlight were definitely not feline. Many of the patients were very fond of the cats and would appear with various inappropriate offerings at feeding time. Not particularly intimidating, you might think, but most of them never said a word and somehow managed to approach without so much as a twig snapping to warn the hapless cat feeder of their presence.

After a few weeks, we pulled ourselves together and most of us burbled merrily to cats and to patients without any expectation of a response from either.

Meanwhile, we had ordered a humane cat trap and were looking forward to embarking on a neutering programme with all the confidence of the totally uninitiated. When this impressive item was delivered, a group of us peered at it knowingly and one or two of us – possibly the men, but my memory could be playing tricks – made comments, such as, 'I thought it might be more complicated,' and, 'I don't think we'll need the instructions…'.

After a couple of hours of merry fumbling – or possibly some fairly brutal exchanges – we looked at the instructions and realised we had been in error. Apparently, the cat was expected to enter at the *other* end of the trap, which would explain why we were puzzled about the location of the spring-loaded platform. Having overcome this difficulty, we then entered upon a lively debate about the operation of said platform, again having recourse to the instructions only when we had exhausted the potential for amusement and a few glasses of El Plonko were sounding like a more attractive option than crouching round a steel trap in the gathering gloom.

A few evenings later, we were galvanised into action by a report from the hospital that one of the ferals had an injured leg which immediately awarded this lucky feline the dubious opportunity to become our first victim. Four of us arrived under cover of darkness and as a stealthy and silent approach is recommended, made sure that each of us managed to trip over a tree root, bash the trap into the back of a fellow-trapper's leg or drop the can of pilchards.

We were fortunate that this particular feral colony was pretty used to our clumsiness and general incompetence by this stage and was waiting patiently for us to stop larking around and get on with dishing up the food. The fact that we seemed determined to make use of this strange equipment was odd, but they were prepared to show a polite interest – as long as the food appeared sooner rather than later.

Predictably, there was no sign initially of the cat with the injured leg, but just as we were dithering about, our quarry obligingly made an appearance. We felt a glow of complacency and baited the trap with irresistible pilchard mush. The cat approached as we melted back into the bushes, limped round the trap, shoved an uninjured leg through in a vain attempt to get his paw on the bait and sat down by the entrance.

I would like to say that we all kept calm. To their eternal credit, three members of the quartet behaved impeccably; I did not. At the sight of the cat so nearly in the trap, I lunged forward with a view to giving him an encouraging shove. It will come as no surprise when I tell you that this did not work. Worse than it not working was the fact that our target shot away with remarkable speed and it was pretty clear that he was unlikely to reappear before midnight. Nobody regretted my foolishness more than I did, but competition for the title of who regretted it most was fierce and my companions spared no effort in trying to snatch it from me.

'What made you think that would be a good idea?' they hissed. 'You're the one who's been saying we must be patient, then you hurl yourself at the poor bloody cat as if you're going for the rugby tackle of your career!'

There was nothing I could say to redeem myself and the folly of my action haunted me for a long time.

However, the evening wasn't a total failure because as we were indulging ourselves in all this fairly well-mannered berating and hand wringing, another cat obligingly nipped into the trap, trod on the spring-loaded platform and down came the trap door. Our initial euphoria took a bit of a knock when we realised we would now have to do something with the cat – as well as panic, that is.

In case you should think we were completely stupid (we were), I should make it clear that we had taken the precaution of arranging to take the injured cat to a local vet, so we covered the trap with an old blanket, as per the instructions, to quieten our prisoner and off we went. I cannot tell you how thrilled the vet was to see us and a feral cat – all of us covered in pilchards and tomato sauce – at the end of a long hard day.

We had thought he would immediately extract the little cat, probably not cuddle it, but certainly speak soothingly to it, before settling it for the night in a cosy kennel. What he did, which is of course the only thing he could possibly do with a wild animal, was carry the trap through to a draught-free corner and push us out into the street as he turned out the lights and locked the door. He would spay the cat tomorrow and nick her left ear so that it would be clear to all that she had been neutered and she wouldn't be subjected to the trauma of being trapped and undergoing an unnecessary operation in the future.

By now, a glass of El Plonko wasn't just a pleasant thought – it was a desperate need and as we relaxed we each remembered what the vet had said about cutting the poor cat's ear.

'Do you think that's really needed? We'll know she's been 'done' won't we? I think we should phone him in the morning and tell him we don't want him to cut her ear.'

'I don't know – we don't want to upset him, do we? She won't know anything about it, will she? It's only the tip of the ear, surely. It won't affect her hearing or anything, will it?'

Exhaustion and El Plonko eventually put paid to our meanderings and by the next morning we were slightly more rational – not to mention under pressure to go to our various places of work and try to behave like normal people.

It had been agreed that I would collect the cat and keep her overnight, then as long as she seemed to be well enough, I would take her back to the colony and release her. I duly collected her and stifled a cry of dismay when I beheld this crumpled little creature in the corner of the trap, crouching on soiled newspaper, with her side shaved and stitched (with soluble sutures) and a pad of blood reddened cotton-wool adhering to the remains of her left ear. She seemed to be so much smaller than the vibrant little white and tortoiseshell cat that popped into the trap the night before; smaller and dispirited.

This was the time for a steady nerve and a professional approach. Unfortunately, I had neither and kept lifting the blanket up to see how our little waif was doing. The vet had given me a stiff talking to about not letting her escape from the trap. I could raise the end piece slightly to slide in a saucer of water and a few morsels of food, but removal of soiled paper was ruled out as being too risky a manoeuvre.

After a sleepless night, I prepared to load the trap into the car and drive little Sophie – for Sophie she had become – to re-join her colony. I gathered together all sorts of delicious offerings that I would dish up for her and her mates to celebrate her homecoming; everything would be fine.

CHAPTER TWO

Sophie and Purrdie – My First 'Wildies'

Purrdie

It will come as no surprise to you to hear that I didn't make that journey. Why I gave that little feral cat a name, I'll never know because any sensible person would know that naming any creature is a gigantic leap down the road to madness. Releasing a wild cat to take its chance living rough is one thing; sending a little cat called Sophie out into what could be a very inhospitable world is entirely another.

I intended to tame this little orphan and she would soon

realise how much happier she was with all the food she could eat, a cosy bed – or umpteen cosy beds – and all the love she needed, rather than running wild in the hospital grounds with all the dangers that lurked there. I decanted her from the trap into a large kitten pen which I'd erected in the kitchen and watched as she scuttled into the soft pink igloo bed.

I didn't see her properly for several days and was worried because although the food was disappearing overnight, there was no sign of any dirt tray activity. When I did eventually see her, I was thrilled to see that her white fur was gleaming and her tortoiseshell patches were once again swirls of vibrant colour. The vet had been quite decisive about the ear clip, taking off considerably more than I had anticipated, but I decided that it actually lent her a rakish charm; this was just as well, of course, as barring prohibitively expensive plastic surgery there was nothing I could do about it.

Sophie had tortoiseshell ears and a dark tortie tail, a scattering of patches on her back and the rest of her coat was a sparkly white, like the surface of fresh snowfall immediately before it melts.

The mystery of the empty dirt tray was solved quite rapidly when the most ghastly smells emanated from the pink igloo which Sophie now refused to sleep in. I was so relieved she wasn't ill that the trashing of a new cat bed seemed a very small price to pay.

She wasn't at all fazed by the other cats in the household, but she remained unimpressed with the silly human who kept talking to her and trying to get her to take food from the hand. After a couple of weeks I opened the door of the kitten pen, having secured the windows, doors and cat flap, but Sophie showed no inclination to venture forth. At night, however, it was a very different story. I would lie in bed, listening to various crashes and ripping noises, punctuated by the occasional spit and growl where the new girl had obviously invaded another resident's territory. Come the morning, she would either be back in the pen or ensconced behind the sofa, with only a trail of fallen pot plants and other wreckage to testify to the activities of our nocturnal marauder.

I felt enormously flattered when Sophie condescended to acknowledge my existence. I don't mean that she sprang on to my lap and purred lovingly; the acknowledgement, when it eventually came, involved glaring at me as if I had two heads, but I chose to see it as preferable to being totally ignored.

It was a long time before I felt confident enough to let her out and when I did fling the patio door open it was with considerable trepidation. I was delighted when she pottered in and out instead of heading for the woods and made sure she was banged up before dusk – the time when all self-respecting cats, feral or otherwise, feel that honour must be served by legging it into the unknown to hunt mice, remains of takeaways or abandoned socks.

In due course it became obvious that Sophie was not exactly a born hunter. Although she had never been handled, she had been part of a well-established and well-fed colony. I also suspect that her predominantly white colour scheme was against her in terms of sneaking up on things. She did, however, have one speciality and, unfortunately, this speciality was sand lizards – one of the rarer species to inhabit this part of the world. Foolishly, the sand lizards had developed a fondness for the border under the window, so it wasn't too taxing for a small and rather amateurish hunter to grab them as they went about their mysterious reptilian business.

In many instances the lizards got away, leaving Sophie clutching a small wriggling tail in her eager paws. As time went on and she became adept at popping through the cat flap, she brought these trophies into the kitchen to be admired and treasured, always announcing her arrival with loud and rather unnerving yodelling noises.

On one occasion the postman – never a barrel of laughs – rather rashly popped a small parcel through the cat flap and inadvertently put his hand on a wriggling lizard tail. I still think the fuss he made was an overreaction.

It took Sophie a good year to settle, but although she never became easy to handle we did reach the stage where – with a determined effort – I could pick her up. The language was pretty appalling (Sophie's as well as mine), but I could at least get her to the vet when the need arose. I can't tell you how thrilled he was to be presented with a feral cat that ripped him to pieces and left steaming deposits on the pristine white table. I wish I could say he made the best of things, but I soon realised that our visits coincided with him being called away to deal with an emergency elsewhere and it would be some unfortunate locum who was left to grapple with Sophie, her semi-hysterical owner and more tail-end mess than you would imagine could possibly come out of such a small cat.

Although Sophie eventually decided that she could just about put up with me, she refused to soften in her attitude to the human race in general. Her reaction to visitors took the form of a non-violent protest and involved crashing out through the flap as soon as they arrived and fleeing down the garden. This worked best when it was lashing with rain, when guests would be treated to the sight of a tiny bedraggled cat coming towards the patio door, seeing that they were still ensconced on the sofa, and rushing back to crouch under the dripping trees. Understandably, most visitors decided that they couldn't possibly stop for a second cup of tea.

Sophie had been with me for some time when another little female cat came into my care. She wasn't exactly feral, but she wasn't exactly domesticated either and her wild side was the one she chose to present on arrival at Tresta Towers. Purrdie, as she became – for no good reason, because purring wasn't high on her agenda – was a small brindle tortoiseshell.

Her rich autumnal colouring was glorious to behold – on the rare occasions we saw her.

I took the decision early on to bring her straight into the house because as Homing Officer for Woking branch of Cats Protection, I knew from experience that poor little Purrdie would struggle to find a home. Cats that hid under blankets and tiddled themselves when anybody looked at them rarely found favour with prospective owners and Purrdie had medals for hiding and tiddling. She was extremely nervous and would have remained in the cat pen, unwanted and unloved, while any number of more confident cats and kittens went on their way with a merry flick of the tail and very definitely without a backward glance.

I installed her under the dining table with all the necessary facilities and there she stayed for a very long time. As Sophie had done before her, she undertook nocturnal expeditions and during the course of these ramblings she formed two significant relationships. She fell in love with Gerbil – a sweet and friendly tabby boy – and was bullied mercilessly by dear little Sophie.

Foolishly, I had expected the two wildies to form a sisterly bond, but Sophie made very sure that Purrdie was aware of their relative places in the pecking order with a relentless regime of lunging runs and tooth-loosening smacks, accompanied by the sort of wailing that would make a banshee seem muted.

About six months after Purrdie's arrival, I had day surgery on my foot and was quite challenged in the mobility department for a while. Purrdie, who had never shown the slightest interest in going outside – in fact, she had hardly shown her face at all during daylight hours – chose this time to leg it down the garden and disappear. I did my best to search the matted, bramble-infested wilderness that passes for a 'conservation area', but achieved nothing more positive than perforations and pain from thorns, mosquitoes and stinging nettles. Even on a good day spotting a brindle tortoiseshell that doesn't want to be spotted in an overgrown jungle is likely to be pretty tricky and this was definitely not a good day.

I lurched down the garden twice a day to call and to leave food, but I was far from confident that I would ever see poor little Purrdie again. When ten days had passed and there had been no sightings, my lack of confidence was replaced by a more definite feeling of despair. A few days later a visitor was gazing down the garden and said how strange it was that a small white cat was patrolling up and down by the back fence.

The small white cat was, of course, no other than Sophie and it occurred to me that she could be a cat on a not very praiseworthy mission. Could it possibly be that Purrdie was the other side of the fence and could it possibly be that her caring little sister was making damn sure she didn't return to the bosom of her neurotic and desperate family?

I continued to call and leave mountains of food by the fence and one evening caught sight of Purrdie on the edge of the lawn. Unfortunately, my jubilation was shortlived as Sophie materialised out of thin air and chased her back into the woods. The next evening I banged Sophie up in a bedroom and left the patio door open with a tempting trail of goodies leading into the depths of the bungalow. Purrdie duly appeared, but showed no sign of approaching beyond the edge of the lawn. The frustration was almost unbearable, but at least I knew she was still around and hadn't been eaten by foxes.

Every now and then even cats – by sheer coincidence – do exactly what is wanted and this was one of those rare occasions. Gerbil sauntered out from the bushes, caught a whiff of some yummy offerings and marched unhesitatingly through the patio door, followed with a great deal of hesitation by young Purrdie. I closed the patio door with a flourish, grabbed a large glass of 'medicine' and sobbed with relief.

Purrdie gradually gained in confidence, sustained by her

passion for Gerbil, but would have very little to do with us. One evening our friends Wendy and Martyn came to visit us, accompanied by Martyn's elderly mother – a perfectly pleasant woman, but not a noted cat enthusiast. We had been chatting for a while when we all suddenly realised that Purrdie was sitting on her lap, being stroked in an absent minded fashion. If Martyn's mum had been nursing a panther we wouldn't have been nearly so shocked!

I can only think that it was our visitor's relative indifference to Purrdie that rendered her a safe companion. Our persistent attempts to engage with our strange little brindled bundle were probably the last thing the poor cat wanted.

Sophie predeceased Purrdie by some years and as Sophie aged, her bullying ways mellowed considerably. In her final months Sophie was herself bullied by Lucy – a small black and white feral girl who will feature in a later chapter – and I had to do everything possible to prevent her from worrying my increasingly frail girl whose white coat was still beautiful, but now lacked the snowy lustre of her younger days.

I had Sophie for ten years and she taught me a great deal about the wilder side of cat rescue. She made me realise how important it is to recognise the needs of the animal instead of insisting it renounces its heritage and fits in with our requirements. I like to think that Purrdie and Sophie lived happy lives – they were certainly loved and cared for and probably safer than they would have been living a wild life. I hope I didn't cramp their style –I let them run as free as my nerves would allow and loved to see them roaming in the woods. They are both long gone now, but their wild shadows still warm a sunny autumn afternoon – and they still chase leaves and feathers through my dreams.

CHAPTER THREE

The Railway Children

Paddy

After our initial panicky trapping activity at the hospital, we took a deep collective breath and proceeded to trap, neuter and release feral cats on a reasonably organised basis. We eventually managed to trap the cat with the injured leg and he was adopted by one of the group, living to a ripe old age and wanting for nothing. We also devised a rota to assist with feeding the cats who remained at the hospital. It was time to extend our activities to the other feral gangs lurking on the fringes of downtown Woking.

Trapping cats in the relatively well-populated and safe environment of the hospital grounds was one thing; venturing to the railway embankment late at night was entirely another. One thing I hadn't reckoned with was the heightened emotions inspired by leather gauntlets and boots amongst the inhabitants of this rather eerie, twilight world. Although the town centre was but yards away, the silence was unnerving and the sudden racketing of high speed trains somewhere above our heads absolutely terrifying.

The railway workers were fascinated by our activities. Some were concerned about the cats and fed them generously. Others thought the cats should be left to fend for themselves at best or poisoned at worst. We soon established a nodding acquaintance with most of the men involved and eventually became used to the trains roaring through – after the style of 'Ghost Riders in the Sky', although of Johnny Cash there was no sign.

One cheery soul told me that the railway workers called the highspeed trains, 'the widder-makers' because over the years a number of men had been killed due to the sudden approach of the train. It was certainly a strange phenomenon because the train made a deafening din when it arrived, but there was very little warning that it was on its way and once it had passed, the noise was swallowed up by the night within seconds. The main problem we experienced was the vibration caused by the wretched thing as it hurtled past as this kept triggering the traps, which would slam shut and require yet another climb to the top of the embankment to re-set them.

This colony had frequented the relatively safe area along by the railway for many years. In fact, we suspected that cats had taken up residence there during the war years and had done quite well for themselves as there was a plentiful supply of rodents as well as a rather spasmodic supply of sandwiches, leftovers from the nearby social club and in later years a tantalising selection of takeaway remains. So desirable was this location that a number of pet cats had availed themselves of the facilities and also fraternised enthusiastically with the feral team.

Once again, we organised a feeding rota and gave ourselves a good talking to about being professional. We would do what we were supposed to do; we would trap the cats, have them neutered and put them back. Only if we managed to grab very tiny kittens would we bring them into foster care with a view to taming them and finding homes.

So far, so good. We gave ourselves a good talking to, but somehow people started to talk about 'Sooty' and 'Paddy' and become ridiculously involved in their wild lives. I am, course, talking about the others in this context and am absolutely sure that lying awake all night was nothing to do with worrying about Paddy the black kitten who was resolutely resisting capture.

We worried a lot about the foxes that also frequented the embankment. Although the adult feral cats were more than capable of giving old foxy a good run for his money, there were litters of vulnerable kittens who were often born in inaccessible undergrowth. Before long, various cat cabins and blankets were lowered over the barbed wire fencing – not that we worried, of course.

I was at home on sick leave with a fairly dire stomach bug when the call came. Paddy was in the trap and there was nothing for it but to drag myself into the driving seat and head for the railway. The climb up the embankment assumed the proportions of an assault on Mount Everest in my weakened state, and the slow slither back down with the trap crashing against my legs was even more of a challenge.

Close up I could see that Paddy was way beyond the tiny tameable kitten stage, so the obvious thing to do was to take him to the vet to be neutered, ear-tipped and then release him back into the bosom of his wild family. But I didn't. I took him home and settled him into an outdoor cat pen, from the depths of which he hurled threats and abuse at me, bless his little fuzzy heart.

In due course Paddy was 'adjusted' and I spent a lot of time trying to persuade him that he was much better off with me and could be a house cat if he played his cards right. He didn't find my arguments compelling and after a few weeks I decided to release him to live outside in the garden, with an old rabbit hutch for shelter and a veritable running buffet of yummy dishes night and morning.

It was unfortunate, to put it mildly, that within hours of me opening the door of the pen my next-door-but-one neighbour saw fit to hold a firework party that transformed our quiet road into a war zone, scaring the living daylights out of all of us and the cats in particular. Of black Paddy there was no sign.

I had a terrible night, tottering out into the garden every hour or so to see if there was any sign of the fugitive. The acrid smell of spent fireworks was heavy on the damp air and as I stood there I was aware that murderous thoughts were coming thick and fast. I lingered over the prospect of lashing my thoughtless neighbour to a large rocket and lighting the blue touch paper with a merry quip. Possibilities included, 'You're fired!' or 'You've always been a high flier'.

The first shaky fingers of dawn were prodding the sky and casting strange shadows around the garden. The birds sounded unnervingly cheerful; how dare they? I wandered round the lawn, thankful that no-one would be looking out of their windows at this time as the sight of a plump, distressed woman in a voluminous nightdress would have been more than enough to trigger a whole galaxy of serious mental health conditions.

As I approached a deep patch of blackness at the bottom of

the cedar tree, I was startled by sudden and extremely indignant hissing. Not many shadows do that; Paddy had come back.

By now, relationships with the railway cats were developing at a rate of knots. A particular bond had been forged between one of our trusty band of feeders and an extremely glamorous tabby cat with a face that could have graced a thousand chocolate boxes. This beautiful cat had a graceful plumed tail, which she knew how to flaunt to maximum effect. She looked fragile, but to survive amongst the foxes, rats and a considerable volume of jettisoned rubbish she must have been tougher than old boots and many times smarter. Unsurprisingly, she became known as 'Fluffy'.

Although we had tried to make the environment more hospitable, the railway embankment was still a very dangerous place for new-born kittens and we were delighted when we managed to get our hands on a heavily pregnant cat and incarcerate her in one of the cattery-style pens I had in the garden. I would like to say she was grateful, but that would be a fib. Her language was quite appalling and her respect for her accommodation somewhere minus zilch.

She was conspicuously unimpressed by the notion of depositing pees and plops in the pink dirt tray I lodged in a private corner of the pen, preferring to perform in the deepest recesses of the cat house and involve as much bedding as possible in the process. Removing such deposits required nerves of steel as well as long arms and a strong stomach. Suffice it to say, one did one's best, but standards slipped in the face of spirited resistance from our little mother-to-be. This consisted of sustained growling, flattened ears, stamping and spitting and I for one found her arguments pretty damn convincing.

One morning I went out to the cat pens and realised that Mumpuss had given birth because she failed to appear in the doorway of the house and I could hear strange noises coming from within. It was some time before I knew that she had produced three kittens and when I eventually saw them I very nearly had kittens myself.

There was one black kitten, one tiny tabby who looked exactly like Mumpuss and a Siamese. I would never have believed it if they hadn't been banged up in a cat pen under lock and key. To those innocent readers (assuming there may be one or two such people!) who believe that cats subscribe to the sanctity of marriage – forget it. The proof, if proof were needed, was before me in that cat pen. Mumpuss had obviously been spoilt for choice when it came to suitors and had played fast and loose with their affections, the result being that at least one of her kittens was likely to have been sired by a cat with a name like Ho Ming Chow.

For a long time we had realised that the regular feeding and relative shelter of the embankment had attracted a transient population of visiting cats, many of whom probably had perfectly good homes but were looking for a few extras in terms of meals and other commodities. We had never seen a Siamese cat in these unlikely surroundings, but the evidence of an oriental liaison was wobbling about before my very eyes.

The black boy and male Siamese lookalike grew rapidly and I made sure that I handled them all from the earliest possible opportunity, which in practical terms meant as soon as Mumpuss began to lose interest in the youngsters so that I could pick them up with a reduced risk of having my face rearranged. The little tabby girl was a fairy-like creature – mouth-wateringly pretty with beautiful markings and as light as a bird. She was a lively little girl and more than held her own with her two boisterous brothers, but it did concern me that she just didn't seem to grow.

This was all a very long time ago and the cats and kittens in our care then were not subjected to the rigorous veterinary checks that are routine these days. We had very little money and simply did the best we could. In the majority of cases, the cats and kittens we homed were healthy, but every now and then there would inevitably be problems. Even with every vet check known to man there could still be problems – I think it's called 'life'.

Anyway, the upshot was that we found homes for all three kittens, but it wasn't long before I had a phone call from the worried owner of the tabby girl, now known as Humbug. After extensive tests, the vet advised that the kitten's diaphragm was incomplete and her stomach was in her chest cavity, leaving no room for her tiny lungs to function effectively.

Drastic problems call for drastic solutions; the vet was very motivated to do his best to save Humbug and the family who had adopted the tiny scrap were pledged to do anything they could to give her a chance of life. We were all of the same mind and somehow the money was raised to finance the operation – which the wonderful vet agreed to carry out at a drastically reduced fee.

It was a massive operation to be performed on such a very small creature and for several days Humbug's life hung in the balance. There were problems – unsurprisingly – with her breathing and she was being fed with a syringe in a desperate bid to keep her strength up. Her owners were at their wits' end and so were we.

Late one evening my phone rang and when I picked it up all I could hear was a woman sobbing. I knew then that tiny Humbug had lost her battle for life. When the sobbing abated, I tried desperately to make sense of what the caller was saying.

'She's eating! She's bloody well eating! Humbug's off the drip and she's bloody well eating!'

This announcement was followed by a crescendo of nose-blowing, followed by more sobbing and more incoherent ramblings – but perhaps that was me.

Mumpuss was spayed and returned to the embankment, looking considerably shinier than she had at the time of her incarceration, but not, I regret to say, more cheerful.

CHAPTER FOUR

Shortleat

Brocky and Elizabeth

For some quite inexplicable reason, the sight of Paddy roaming around my garden was such a joy that I began to think it would be no bad thing to have more feral cats, should the opportunity arise. They would live their lives as free spirits – fed and sheltered spirits, that is – but I wouldn't attempt to domesticate them.

When word came from the railway embankment that there was growing concern in some quarters about the number of cats living there, I had a sudden intimation of what Joan of Arc went through with all that stuff about voices. Someone was obviously telling me that the time was right to increase my own little feral colony.

The next cat to be trapped was a very pretty little black and white girl, who went into the trap quietly enough and transformed herself into tornado within seconds of the trap clanging shut. In fact, her reaction was so extreme that it frightened the other ferals, who legged it into the undergrowth. All except one – a large black and white male cat who was doing everything within his power to get inside the trap. We set another trap as fast as our shaky, pilchard-covered fingers would allow and the boy rushed in; I don't think we entirely imagined a look of considerable relief on his big tomcat face as he did so.

These two cats didn't have the total wildness exhibited by most of the railway cats and it seemed likely that the female in particular could have been a pet at some stage. I decided that these two would grace the grounds of Tresta Towers and be appropriate friends for Paddy, who they might even remember as an erstwhile resident of Railway Cuttings.

I kept Lucy and Brocky in a cat pen for several weeks after neutering and spaying, then on a quiet sunny morning, having spitefully withheld breakfast, I propped the door open. Watching from behind the garage, I saw big Brocky emerge hesitantly, then like a rapidly uncoiling spring he flew down the garden and leapt the six-foot fence, his paws hardly touching the top as he dropped out of sight into dense woodland. How many humans would be able to sprint and leap like that after being incarcerated in a small pen for several weeks? I've only got to get up from the sofa a bit too quickly to pull several muscles and sprain an ankle.

Optimism is a key requirement for anybody involved in animal rescue, so I was immediately convinced that I would never clap eyes on Brocky's big silly piebald face again. My first thought was to close the pen door to keep Lucy safe, but I realised that if by any remote chance Brocky should return, a closed door would hardly be a welcoming gesture. I wandered in the woods for most of the afternoon – a pathetic, wailing figure; my only achievement was to scare several dog-walkers and their pooches, and put the fear of God up a young couple who certainly weren't walking dogs or looking for mushrooms.

Once darkness rendered further woodland rambling downright dangerous, I contented myself with furtive visits to the pen. There was no sign of Brocky, but Lucy was still sitting it out in her bed at the back of the cat house, obviously blaming me for everything. I tottered out in the early hours and Lucy had gone. I was actually quite relieved, because at least there was a very good chance that she would find him, even if I never saw either of them again. By this time I was convinced they were mother and son – or possibly, husband and wife, but in cat circles these are just words.

It was around nine o'clock the following morning when two black and white cats soared over the back fence and trotted across the lawn. They didn't exactly fling themselves into my arms, but the look on their faces conveyed the message that they were hungry and could I please stop gawping at them in that ridiculous fashion and get them some food.

Lucy and Brocky lived with me for years. They were quite happy in their cat chalet in the garden until one particularly chilly winter's evening they thought better of it and moved indoors. This decision made, there was no hesitancy about claiming a cosy billet on a suitably padded armchair, where they curled up together after helping themselves to the running buffet in the kitchen. None of the domestic cats took any notice because, of course, they already knew them from their garden excursions and walls never have meant anything to any self-respecting cat.

Lucy could only have been about ten years old when her wonderfully lustrous black coat began to lose its glorious sheen and even her white paws and bib were not as spotless as before. It wasn't long before she began to lose weight and blood tests revealed serious kidney problems. I did my best with medication and special diets, but her time had come and she slipped away to the Great Dirt Tray in the Sky. Poor Brocky was bereft, but not for long. He turned his attention to my dear old grey and white boy, Malcolm, and if Malcolm wasn't altogether comfortable with the idea of being padded and prodded by an extremely large and simple boy cat, he was far too polite to show it. After dear Malcolm headed for his own fluffy and permanently sunblessed cloud, it took Brocky only a few days to realise that Elizabeth should be his new best friend. It took Elizabeth rather longer to adjust to the idea, but in the end they were inseparable.

While Lucy and Brocky were settling in at Tresta Towers we suddenly heard rumours about the hospital site, where there were still quite a number of ferals, being sold off to developers and within an alarmingly short time the rumours were confirmed. The pressure was on to relocate the colony and it was all hands to the cat traps. We did pretty well at this and the unsurprising result was that I ended up with two more candidates for the Tresta Towers commune.

They were still kittens when they arrived: a fuzzy black boy and a shorthaired tabby and white lad. Their language was appalling and they gave no indication that they felt even a twinge of gratitude. The fluffy boy soon became 'Tufty' and – for absolutely no logical reason at all – his companion was called 'Dennis'. I have no idea whether or not they were brothers, but I liked to think so.

I kept them in a cat pen until they were old enough to be neutered and released them shortly after. By now I had several cat chalets in a sheltered corner of the garden – a miniature village which soon became known as 'Kitty City'. Tufty and Dennis soon settled in, establishing good relationships with the other ferals and with the domestic residents.

At this time Lucy and Brocky were still enjoying the best of both worlds, spending their time outside when the weather was good – or possibly when there wasn't much on the telly. They were still part of the feral gang, hanging around with Paddy and tolerating the newcomers without so much as a grumble, but they were fair-weather ferals and came indoors at the first hint of a chilly breeze. My elderly father was enraged by their behaviour, telling me repeatedly that they were 'takers, not givers' and it was a one-sided relationship. It was pointless to tell him that cats are not like dogs; that true cat lovers glory in the cat's independence and even in its selfishness!

Around this time I heard about Skippy, a young adult feral cat that was living rough not far from the hospital grounds. He was mainly white with rather strange tabby markings and certainly lived up to his name. When he left the cat pen he ran round and round the garden, then disappeared. I didn't see him for some days, but eventually caught a glimpse of his little white face emerging from under the summerhouse. This was his retreat for some time, but eventually he made the move into the superior accommodation of Kitty City.

By now the established colonies were fairly stable as our trapping and neutering activities had paid dividends. Young kittens were taken, tamed and found homes and regular feeding was arranged for the remaining neutered adults.

This didn't mean the end of the feral problem, of course. Even now it saddens me that so many cat owners show a lamentable lack of responsibility as far as their pets are concerned, abandoning them whenever life takes an unexpected or a challenging turn.

The population of Kitty City gradually expanded with the arrival of Spitfire, a fierce black girl, who arrived as a tiny kitten but refused to have anything to do with this taming business. Her sister and brother were quick to see the benefits of abandoning their wildness and throwing in their lot with some suitably besotted humans, but Spitfire remained resolutely unimpressed. She enjoyed the company of the others, but I was convinced that she really needed a companion nearer her own age. Delilah would be the solution to the problem.

Delilah's mother was almost certainly a victim of a failed human relationship as well as a failed feline one (unsurprisingly there was no sign of the kittens' father) and found herself homeless, pregnant and starving in what would be regarded as a 'rather nice' area. In due course this poor little cat produced three kittens – unfortunately in the garden of a woman who made the witches in *Macbeth* seem cuddly.

This impressively ghastly woman phoned me, insisting that I come and remove the cats immediately if not sooner, but also insisting that she couldn't possibly give me access to her house or garden. Spot the difficulty!

In due course, I trapped the mother and her three beautiful kittens – one shorthaired ginger boy and two longhaired tortoiseshell girls. I decided to keep one of the girls – Delilah – as she was easily the wildest of the kittens. The other members of her extraordinarily good-looking family found excellent homes and settled well.

Spitfire and Delilah bonded immediately. During the time that Delilah was in the cat pen, Spitfire would sit outside and once her friend was old enough to be spayed and released the two of them became inseparable, chumming up with Lynx, our little tabby wildie.

Nobody glimpsing a tiger in a distant jungle could have relished the sighting more than I relished seeing these magnificent wild cats soaking up the last rays of sun on a summer's evening in the overgrown tangle of my own back garden.

Delilah

Dennis

Lynx

Tufty

CHAPTER FIVE

Adventures in the Wilds of Surrey

As civilisation marches relentlessly across the planet, the truly wild places are disappearing at an alarming rate. Parts of the Amazon Basin still have their moments, of course, and I have it on good authority that there are expanses of desert where you can wander for days without seeing anything more companionable than a sulky camel.

It is not generally realised that there are places in Surrey which are quite possibly the wildest of the lot.

Cat rescuers pride themselves on responding to the call, but as I shoved three large traps and two cat carriers into my trusty Honda Civic, I couldn't help reflecting that both the car and I would be better suited to pottering off to Sainsbury's than flinging ourselves across fields that a steeplechaser would jib at crossing.

A frequent feature of trapping in such places is a requirement to rendezvous with a contact in order to be escorted to the secret location where the wild cats live. It goes without saying that the contact will not be in the car for which you have details because their wife, husband or possibly dog needed to use it. The lane you have arranged to meet them in will inevitably have no landmarks and after driving up and down it countless times you won't have a clue whether to look for them on the left or the right. By this point, you are likely to be overcome with pilchard fumes and/or garlic sausage from the intended bait and the initial meeting could be less than amicable.

The Ockham experience started surprisingly well with the contact arriving in the right make of car. It was blue, not silver, but it would have been churlish to quibble over details. We lurched off into the middle of nowhere – rather more speedily than I would have chosen to, encumbered as I was with rattling traps and flying pilchards – but I was terrified I would lose sight of my guide, so rammed my foot down and prayed.

The wild ones were desperately hungry, aggressive and breathtakingly beautiful. For years they had been fed by a kind and totally batty old man living in a cottage nearby, but sadly he had died and it had been a while before anybody had realised what was going on.

We got off to an excellent start with a lovely, but intellectually challenged, grey youngster strolling into an ordinary front-loading cat carrier and being unceremoniously banged up. This was going to be a piece of cake!

An attempt to catch a sharp little tortoiseshell number failed spectacularly with her heading off at speed in the general direction of Edinburgh. Neatly coinciding with this downturn in our fortunes, a thoroughly objectionable woman appeared from nowhere and asked us to account for our actions. She also demanded to know whether 'Ted' knew what was going on, insisting on carrying out the interrogation at maximum volume.

As murderous thoughts were coursing through my brain, Ted appeared, driving across the fields at a speed which would not have been out of place in a Formula One race. He explained that he had been feeding the cats after their benefactor's death, but had no wish to continue doing so and would be pleased to see them caught, neutered and only returned if suitable homes couldn't be found for them.

Far from being alarmed by Ted's noisy arrival, the cats re-appeared and we had three adults in traps in no time, including a rather clueless ginger and white boy who couldn't fling himself in quickly enough. When I looked around for the dreadful woman she had either beaten a retreat or changed into a rather stunted tree.

The whole episode was typical of trapping – long periods of boredom, punctuated by brief moments of frenzied activity or panic. We were now left with the naughty tortie baby who was busy chasing leaves, her tail and the occasional blundering moth.

I felt very uneasy about leaving her behind, but we couldn't linger much longer as the cats we'd already caught needed to be decanted into cat pens and the prospect of finding our way back to the road in failing light without wrecking the car was a worrying one. While I was grappling with this dilemma, Ted turned in an instant from gruff stranger into Superman and grabbed the kitten by the scruff of the neck. It was an uneven struggle – a fully grown man versus a small kitten – but surprisingly Ted won, losing no more than a couple of pints of blood in the process.

Of course it isn't fair that fortune favours the beautiful, but that is the way of the world and never more so than in cat rescue. The cats we brought away from Ockham were very beautiful and after a short time revealed that they weren't quite as feral as early impressions led us to believe. The colony had been fed regularly and had therefore been accustomed to the looming clumsiness of human beings, and this was no doubt a major factor in the taming process. They all found homes apart from a couple of adults that we succeeded in relocating to a riding stables, where they shook up the local rodent population – when they weren't mopping up tasty treats provided by an army of young riders.

There is a lot of common land in Surrey. Looking at an ordnance survey map could give you the impression that the area is criss-crossed by roads and bridleways to the extent that it would be impossible to escape the straggling tendrils of the civilised world. Do not believe it! I can personally vouch for the fact that there are areas within a very short distance of Tresta Towers that would have Bear Grylls feeling isolated.

A strange phenomenon about working with feral cats is that quite often the cats are the least of the problem. The very person who has demanded you leap into action immediately to deal with the burgeoning cat problem is very likely to be the person who makes the task extremely difficult to achieve – if not downright impossible.

Suffice it to say that we were called upon to catch between twenty and thirty ferals, have them neutered and return them to a farm which I shall call Withering Sleights to protect the guilty. To reach the farm it was necessary to navigate a complex web of winding, muddy lanes riddled with enormous pot holes. Even on a sunny day there was a disconcerting chill about the place and a dampness underfoot that became a pungent river of cow manure in wet weather.

As we lugged six traps into a vast barn, numerous feline shadows melted behind the straw bales, but we had seen enough to realise that the original estimate could be on the low side. The majority of the cats were tabby, with a few black cousins. It would be essential to have them ear-clipped or we would be forever trapping and carting off the same cats; experience had shown that some cats would wander into a trap again within days of what one would think of as a traumatic episode, while other, more canny felines would give the threatening steel traps a wide berth from Day One.

We started well. With a total of six traps in operation we caught seven cats – two having decided to squeeze in together – within thirty minutes. These were whisked away to be 'adjusted' and brought back the following day.

We did well on the next few visits, but inevitably the remaining cats became more wary and we were sometimes braving the waterlogged lanes and pot holes and hanging around for a couple of hours only to come away empty handed.

Up until now, the lady farmer had pretty well left us to get on with things, which was fine, but she suddenly decided to intervene – and not in a good way. At 4.30 pm she emerged from the ancient farmhouse, clad in pyjamas and pink slippers, and without acknowledging our presence in any way scampered into the barn. She then proceeded to scatter food all over the barn floor and into the traps we had so carefully baited. If any cat showed any sign of entering the trap, she would rush up behind it, ensuring that it rushed in the opposite direction as fast as it could go.

The woman, quite frankly, was a cat trapper's nightmare. After a few more weeks she suddenly told us we were banned from her property. By this time we had succeeded in neutering a large number of cats, but we were disappointed (to put it mildly!) that we were unable to finish the job. We knew only too well that with a small number of unspayed females and a couple of entire tom cats still on the scene there would soon be more hungry and inbred kittens in a world that already has more than its fair share of misery.

I can only say that we did our best and as far as one weedy little kitten was concerned, we didn't do too badly at all. He really was a poor little scrap and to return him to the farm after his neutering operation would almost certainly have resulted in his death. I kept him in a cat pen so that he could recover in comfort and safety and somehow it slipped my mind to take him back.

The hardest lesson to learn with this sort of assignment is that total success is often beyond one's reach. There are factors beyond the rescuer's control, such as difficult (understatement!) people and restricted access, but the important thing is to do whatever is possible to reduce the suffering and misery to innocent animals.

I shall always regret the fact we were unable to help every cat at Withering Sleights, but we did help a great many and I happen to know that one little scrap of a kitten is now a sleek and much-loved cat, ruling his slaves with a benevolent and velvety paw.

CHAPTER SIX

Relocating Feral Cats

The best advice that anybody could give about relocating feral cats is don't – unless there is absolutely no way that they can be trapped, neutered and returned to their familiar surroundings.

The main difficulty in my experience about moving wild cats to a new location is being able to contain them for long enough for them to familiarise themselves with their new territory. Even if this can be achieved, there remains the challenge of other predators, who are unlikely to welcome a new arrival with unbounded enthusiasm, and the human-generated hazards such as cars, rubbish, pesticides and over-enthusiastic clearance of wild spaces that could provide a handy home for a wild creature.

Occasionally, however, the original situation is so ghastly that there really is no option but to seek a new placement for the endearing little creature that wants nothing more than to rip your throat out at the time of capture.

An interesting feature of involvement in cat rescue is that the general public tend to assume the rescuer has superhuman powers. As a short, overweight, middle aged woman I have been asked on numerous occasions why I am not prepared to climb a tall spindly tree to rescue a kitten that will almost certainly make its own way down if left to its own devices; disappointment has also been expressed at my unsporting attitude to running round a large graveyard to catch a cat that had voted with his paws when it was time to visit the vet.

Obviously this peevish reluctance to go the extra mile calls into question my dedication to the cause.

Sometimes, however, I have had no option but to undertake what to me has been a fairly hazardous venture when relocating feral cats.

I was awaiting a hip replacement when a kind farmer agreed to take a small black and white feral girl who had been found in an inhospitable back street. She was well and truly wild with a healthy loathing for the human race. I suspect she had no reason to like us, but I found her reactions a trifle wounding, muttering as she spat at me various rebukes along the lines of, 'Don't be grateful – I'm only trying to help you! I don't expect you to purr, but not ripping me to pieces would be good.'

Although I was a bit dodgy on my pins at the time, I was able to cope with normal activities and set off for the farm feeling quietly confident. I'd packed the trusty kitten pen, in which little Rosie would spend about three weeks settling into her new environment before being released to roam and along the way polish off a few rodents. I would carefully decant her from the carrier into the pen and be home in time for a relaxing Sunday lunch.

The woman farmer was all smiles, and ushered me towards a large airy barn where Rosie would be based. She carried the pen and I carried Rosie, who amused herself by jabbing me in the leg at frequent intervals.

'Right,' I said, glancing round the extensive barn, 'where had you thought of having the pen?'

'I thought she'd be happiest up there,' she said, indicating a mountain of straw bales with an airy wave.

I could see the sense in this because in the dark reaches of the night, who knew what inquisitive dogs or foxes might come sniffing around and poor little Rosie would feel horribly vulnerable trapped in her kitten pen, even if they didn't stand a chance of getting her. What was less clear to me was how I would get the pen and cat to the top of Straw Mountain without Rosie escaping or me breaking my leg.

To be fair to my companion, she was quick to offer to go up herself and install Rosie in her bijou residence, but here we stumbled against another interesting feature of cat rescue: the conceited idea that most rescuers have that they and they alone are the only ones who can do anything. Actually, this isn't just big headedness, because feral cats can pack quite a punch which can come as a surprise to those more closely acquainted with the tea cosy variety. There is also the feeling that however badly these wildies have behaved, they are our responsibility until safely released or relocated.

The result of all this was that I found myself clambering upwards with the poor woman holding my legs and passing things to me as I wavered precariously on the pile of straw. Rosie, meanwhile, fidgeted up and down in the carrier so that it crashed into my legs and when that failed to send me plummeting, shoved her paw through the grill so that she could rake her claws playfully down the back of my leg. Whatever failings ferals have, they could never be accused of being helpful.

With the pen door open and the open cat carrier jammed against it, I felt the usual rush of adrenalin accompanied by a pressing need to get to the loo. This would be a worry at the best of times, but is far from ideal when the unfortunate human is trying to encourage the wild cat to move into a cage while balancing on a pile of straw bales. I would like to say that Rosie co-operated fully in this enterprise, but obviously you wouldn't believe that. What you probably would believe is that dear little Rosie – having loathed the idea of going into the carrier – had now decided that it was the one place in the world that she wanted to be. By the time she condescended to be tipped into the pen, both my arms and my bladder had pretty well given hope.

It's not always so tricky, of course. Sometimes it's just embarrassing, as when I had had the good fortune to find a billet for three needy feral cats at a local riding stables. I set off with a friend to install them in their new home and was delighted to see that a large shed had been earmarked for their initial settling in period. We were confident that the cats would keep away from the door when it was opened to admit the cat feeder, but as an additional safeguard the owner was going to put a board across the bottom half of the door to discourage escapes. My friend and I went in and released the ferals, who promptly shot to the back of the shed to hide. Meanwhile, the stable owner had positioned the board and was poised to shut the door once we had nipped out.

My friend stepped over the board without incident and I prepared to follow, but being quite short there was absolutely no way that I could, as it were, get my leg over. By now one feral was showing rather too much interest in the fresh air and without a word the two women hoisted me over the board and closed the door, with scant regard, it has to be said, for my dignity or wellbeing.

Friends and I have often driven considerable distances to relocate feral cats and inevitably at some point along a traffic-infested motorway with half a dozen ferals peeing and vomiting over the backseat, the thought would occur that there might be jollier ways of spending the day.

Once at the destination, however, the sight of specially constructed pens and cosy bedding would soon cheer things up and I honestly have to say that in my experience and that of my trapper friends it has done our weary hearts the world of good to see how much trouble many people have been prepared to take to give these cats from the wrong side of the tracks another chance of happiness.

Pawnote

Feral cats do tend to be a law unto themselves, but this isn't the main reason for gangs of them being located behind the perimeter fencing of several prisons. Many prisons have major problems with vermin in the form of rats, mice and pigeons and half a dozen neutered and health-checked feral cats provide a relatively cheap alternative to other forms of pest control.

It is important that they are fed regularly and that water is provided, but in most prisons the main problem is to limit the 'extras' provided by prisoners, for whom the cats are a welcome interest and probably a reminder of a home life many have not experienced for a very long time.

Kitty City

CHAPTER SEVEN

Return to the Wild

There obviously couldn't be anything more straightforward than returning a feral cat to its home ground. The cat wants to be free, you want it to be free and all you've got to do is get it there.

Usually the question of handling feral cats doesn't arise because normally the cat would be trapped, taken to the vet's for neutering and ear clipping, popped back into the trap and taken home in the trap. This would generally be achieved within 24 hours. Sometimes, however, the cat is injured, or a pregnancy might be too advanced for the cat to be spayed safely, necessitating a prolonged stay in a cat pen.

Catching a feral cat in a cat pen should be easy. It obviously can't go far and with bite-proof gauntlets, substantial clothing and a dash of commonsense it should be a stroll in the park. Except that some of us have learnt the hard way that even a stroll in the park can be a bit dodgy. For a start, there's the sad old flashers to avoid, not to mention the mums with buggies the size of a large estate car and their generally ghastly children who, when they're not screaming from the depths of their McLaren buggies are very likely to be mowing you down with their dear little bicycles.

But I digress. Back to the feral cats and the joyous experience of catching them by hand – by hand, because the chances of them ever going back into a trap while banged up in a pen are somewhere minus zilch, as I may have observed previously.

However, I can thoroughly recommend the ancient sport of feral catching to anyone who feels that modern life is a bit too tame, with an adrenalin rush guaranteed and quite possibly a trip to A & E.

A bulky old feral rejoicing in the name of Blackie (we really anguished over that one!) was trapped on the campus of a local university after an alarming phone conversation suggesting that his face was likely to explode. He was a mature and extremely smelly tomcat, but the attractive aroma that filled the car on my journey home had the added plus of a discharging abscess with piquant undertones of pilchard, the latter having been the way to Blackie's heart, or – to put it in more basic terms – the only way to get the bugger in the trap.

The pus-filled sack that hung from his poor face was indeed a fearsome sight. The next day, the vet sorted Blackie out, but advised a period of incarceration so that he could be given antibiotics and generally cosseted for a couple of weeks before going home.

Each time I entered the cat pen, Blackie would step forward and growl and spit in the most heart-warming manner, but this was nowhere near as terrifying as the feral stamp. The noise that he made by stamping on the wooden floor of the cat house was incredible bearing in mind that even a large cat has short legs. Another winning trait was Blackie's religious conviction that dirt trays were the work of the devil and must not be used at any price. Over the course of two weeks an impressive haul of deposits had to removed, necessitating some imaginative wielding of kitchen rolls and grabber sticks while keeping a wary eye on the miniature panther in the doorway of the cat house.

The good news was that he wolfed down the crushed tablets in food and at the end of two weeks looked the picture of rude health. I set the trap in the pen, knowing as I did so that I was just going through the motions and would have to catch him by hand.

Sure enough, after a sleepless night I was rewarded by the sight of an empty trap and a smirking cat. Donning the trusty gauntlets and a particularly winning combination of baggy jeans and lurid orange anorak, I entered the arena with much the same misgivings as the Roman gladiators must have experienced as they confronted a bad tempered lion. With trembling hands I raised the open trap to the doorway of the house and unbelievably Blackie strolled in. I shoved the cover in the slots and did what anyone would do in the circumstances – rushed to the loo to chuck up. Relief can do that to a girl!

It's always rewarding when animals seem to realise you've done your best to help them and I would like to say that Blackie blinked at me warmly as he skipped out of the trap on his home turf. Unfortunately – and I'm sure it was just a misunderstanding – he sauntered out of the trap and approached me, coming close enough to deliver a drenching spray of urine over my baggy jeans.

A call to trap and neuter a gang of young ferals in the depths of the Surrey Hills was one of the pleasanter projects I was involved in – not least because the lovely lady who lived there always provided a large plateful of particularly yummy chocolate biscuits which I politely consumed while waiting for the traps to fill. Unfortunately, the cats in question were all around the same size and black, so even with tipped left ears it would have been tricky to identify in failing light which cats had already been neutered. It therefore made sense to bang the youngsters up in a cat pen and return them once they had all been rounded up and dealt with.

In due course, I had five beautiful cats ready to go home and all I had to do was grab them and shove them into top-opening cat carriers. They were small, light cats and although they were terrified, they lacked the passionate hatred of humans so convincingly displayed by dear old Blackie. A friend would be coming to release them with me and the whole enterprise seemed no more than a jolly trip out.

My friend was unavoidably delayed, so I left a note on the door asking her to come round the back as I would be making a start on getting the cats into the carriers. In the time honoured way, I let the cats do a few circuits of the pen before I grabbed anybody so they would be slightly winded. The first 'victim' presented only a token resistance and I turned my attention to the next, who obligingly shot up the wire and clung to the roof. I reached up, failed to get a good grip on his shiny fur and he let go, plummeting towards the floor of the pen and slowing his descent by sliding down the side of my face. He also caught my ear lobe and blood – mine, not his – spurted everywhere.

I dabbed pathetically at my wounds with a microscopic paper tissue, but the sight greeting my traumatised friend was not a pleasant one. I couldn't open the outer door of the pen, of course, or the cats would have legged it – probably never to be seen again – so there was nothing for it but to carry on grabbing while my friend stuffed tissues through the wire and made bracing and rather annoying comments, such as, 'It probably looks worse than it is.'

Eventually we had the carriers jammed into the car and set off – not quite with a song in our hearts, but with the flow of blood slowing to a trickle. The journey was uneventful and the release of the ferals achieved with only a momentary urge on my part to murder the chocolate biscuit provider when she ventured to hope that none of the cats had been injured in the struggle.

The narrow lane back to the main road was filling rapidly with dusky mist and suddenly a stooped figure loomed ahead, accompanied by an enormous Labrador. I couldn't see the dog as it came nearer and was worried sick that I might run the poor thing over, so opened the window – partly to shriek abuse at the moron with it, but also to try and see where the dog was in relation to the wheels of the car. As I peered out, an enormous black head clunked me soundly on the forehead, almost rendering me unconscious.

Ever one for a helpful comment, my companion mused, 'I suppose they're like sharks. He must have smelt blood!'

Rallying, we continued and reached home where a couple of large glasses of El Plonko almost had us seeing the funny side. My friend skipped off and a few minutes later Poor Roger, my long-suffering husband, pulled into the drive. I waved weakly, imagining how concerned he would be when he saw my still quite impressive injuries. The drive, gentle reader, is not a long one and it would take approximately ten seconds to reach the door of Tresta Towers, without breaking into a sweat. When he didn't appear, I flung open the door to see him peering at the car in an anxious manner.

He looked up, totally ignored the congealed blood, and asked me whatever had happened to the car.

'Blige!' he exclaimed (he is from Bristol), 'what happened? How did all this mud get on the car door? I hope it's not scratched! I'll just get changed and wash it off.'

I shall gloss over the interesting and meaningful conversation that followed, but suffice it to say that he decided to delay the car inspection and book a table at a rather pleasant hostelry instead.

CHAPTER EIGHT

Phoney Ferals

Evie

I can remember hanging around on street corners in my teens with some deeply unattractive blokes who had obviously been told by some joker that girls can't resist a tough guy, particularly if he ignores her except when blowing bubble gum over her spectacles. If only someone had told them that this girl would have found it very much harder to resist being taken out for a decent meal by somebody who owned a car which you could sit in without having to hang on to the door in case it fell off.

I can only assume that the same sort of rumours abound

in feline society because my feral adventures included a sprinkling of cats – boys, obviously – who insisted that they were feral, but turned out to be about as tough as particularly soggy mashed potato – although I must admit that some of my granny's lumpy offerings could be fairly challenging.

I have lived for too many years expecting things to go wrong to suddenly develop the sort of happy-go-lucky personality that would set off to trap a feral cat without donning the sort of outfit that would make a cautious bee-keeper seem underdressed and this has led to some embarrassing episodes from time to time.

It was a sunny afternoon in suburbia when I clanked up in full trapping regalia with the steel trap crashing fetchingly against my legs, only to find that there was a children's party in full swing in the back garden. Thinking I must have the wrong address and that they were only smiling because they had mistaken me for the entertainment, I made suitable enquiries.

'Yes, that's right, love. This is the place. Do you want to put that down? It looks a bit heavy and awkward.'

I smiled nervously – a required art for cat rescue work. 'I'm worried we won't see much of the feral cat with all this excitement going on.'

As I spoke, I edged past a large black moggy who was sprawled out by the paddling pool.

'There he is, love! He loves it here! We can't keep him though and he'll get a good home, won't he?'

'But he doesn't seem very *wild*,' I stuttered. 'In fact, he seems more docile than most of the cats I know!'

'He won't like going in that funny old cat cage you've brought, dear. That's why I said he'd be wild. He always gets ever so cross when you put him inside a cage.'

Silly me!

A decent interval after this chastening experience, I was called to trap a delinquent tomcat on a large housing estate and spent a fascinating, if frustrating, afternoon watching a rangy piebald tom circling the cage. I wasn't the slightest bit lonely because it was obviously a slow afternoon on the telly and I ended up with more new friends than I would have thought could ever have emerged from the surrounding houses. I was particularly heartened to see another dog arriving as at one time it looked as if we might only have half-a-dozen.

After a good couple of hours a middle-aged gentleman, who had been with me for the duration of the vigil, suddenly grunted something unintelligible, grabbed the tomcat on one of its circuits, and shoved him in the trap. I didn't know whether to kill the man or shake his hand, but as the nervous smile is my stock in-trade I relied heavily upon it as I lugged the trap to the car.

Being involved in cat trapping activities brings the sort of camaraderie generally felt by groups of people who have gone through some sort of traumatic experience together. There is a sense that other people cannot possibly appreciate what you have been through or understand the boredom, the fear, the triumph, etc, etc, etc; and, of course, it can be quite traumatic: sitting in a car overwhelmed by the combined smells of pilchards and cat pee.

A regular port of call for a long time was the Fish Farm near Wraysbury, where an extended family of the most beautiful cats you could possibly imagine lived out their lives. It was an idyllic situation – dreamy 'Wind in the Willows' riverbanks and velvety, moth-filled summer evenings. The cats were well fed by the owner of the Fish Farm, but as neutering didn't feature on his agenda, we knew that something had to be done or soon you wouldn't be able to put your foot down for cats and kittens and it would all end in tears.

We had a lot of success there because although the cats were pretty wild when we trapped them, even the adults tended to tame quite quickly and they were such glorious colours that we rarely struggled to find homes for them. My theory was that as they were all quite young cats, their immediate ancestors were almost certainly strays rather than real ferals with the wildness of many generations running through their veins.

Having said that, we generally planned to return the older adult cats, secure in the knowledge that they would live out their lives in a safe location and with a plentiful food supply, and so it was that I returned one evening with handsome tabby Mickey, who had given me a good run for my money in the pen and shown a marked inclination to tear my throat out as I rammed him into the carrier.

When we arrived at the Fish Farm, however, Mickey realised how fond he was of the cat carrier and efforts to shake him out did no more than elicit a few flaring spits. After a while, the owner of the Fish Farm decided that he had better things to do than stare at a motionless cat and listen to a strange woman conducting a one-sided conversation about the relative merits of top-loading and front-loading cat carriers. He strolled over, bent down and, completely ignoring the crescendo of growls emanating from the crouching Mickey, picked him up and told him not to be so silly. Not only did he pick him up, but he gave him a manly hug which coaxed a grudging purr out of the feline traitor.

I homed a number of young adults, including a mouth-wateringly beautiful purple grey girl with a coat like satin. Bastet was very nervous and could certainly find it in her heart to bite when handling was on the agenda, but she was young enough and sweet enough to make a pet as long as I could find the right owner – that is somebody who realised she would need time to settle and might never be overwhelmingly friendly to people other than her owners.

A very pleasant couple came to see her and fell for her straight away, saying all the right things about keeping her safe indoors for a long time and not rushing her, and so on the appointed day I arrived with little Bastet. During the short journey to her new home, the sweet cat had burrowed under her blankets and as soon as I opened the carrier she headed for the darkest corner of the room.

I kept in touch and was worried to hear that she wasn't really progressing after some six weeks and they had had to put the dirt tray under the sideboard where she was hiding as she wouldn't come out to use it even if it was only a couple of feet away. They were adamant that they wouldn't give up, but I was beginning to wonder if it wouldn't be fairer to them and their terrified lodger to return her to her wild family.

They phoned me a few days later to tell me they would have to get somebody in to repair the boiler and were worried sick that Bastet would be terrified of all the noise; not only that, they were concerned that the boiler man would leave the door open and that would be that. We agreed that they would have to impress upon him the need for caution and leave notes everywhere reminding him to be careful with doors.

While he was working on the boiler in the inner hall, they had peered under the sideboard to find that Bastet had legged it. Cat lovers are, of course, the most reasonable of people and Bastet's human mother immediately started berating the poor man.

'You must have left the door open! After all we said about the cat and how nervous she is! Well – that's it! We'll never see her again!'

Emerging from the cupboard, the young man replied in a considered manner.

'How many cats have you got then? I thought you'd just got the one.'

'Yes – one grey cat. Why?'

'Because she's here helping me. Dear little thing, isn't she?'

It would have been difficult to call the black stray that arrived a few years ago in the vicinity of Tresta Towers anything but 'Tom'. He so clearly was a tomcat from his John Wayne swagger to his wonderfully jowly face that to call him anything else would have been plain unconvincing. Tom had clearly made up his mind that this was his intended destination – or rather, that the bungalow across the road was.

The remarkable thing about Tom was that he could bide his time. There was no unseemly battering down of cat flaps and he didn't go in for nocturnal disturbances, preferring to target his human quarry with a meaningful stare and a quivering, 'happy tail'. He would stroll through our gardens, acknowledging feline residents with a courteous blink and occasionally a submissive rollover. We always knew when Tom was on his way because we could hear him singing as he arrived – a manly baritone with occasional teeters into a tenor register.

As it became obvious that Tom had no intentions of returning home – mainly because to all intents and purposes he was home – we began to think about rounding him up and getting him checked out and neutered. By now, he had succeeded in his masterplan. Not only was the lovely neighbour across the road willing to take Tom into her home, but she was thrilled to bits that this handsome boy had chosen her. Pausing only to change from skittish feral to couch potato within the space of a few hours, Tom moved in and set about getting things organised. In no time at all, his grizzled charm had worked its magic and at least three meals a day plus fresh chicken snacks were appearing without him needing to raise a paw.

As the day for his trip to the vet drew nearer, Tom chummed up with a pretty little stray tabby girl, who – you've guessed – looked much too young to have kittens, but somehow grew up overnight when Tom made her an offer she just couldn't refuse. The future dynasty secured, Tom could relax.

Missy duly produced a litter of kittens in the woods behind

our row of bungalows and was adopted by our neighbours. Her kittens were re-homed with the help of Cats Protection and Missy wasted no time in making the transition from nervy stray to despotic ruler of besotted humans.

We often see Tom making his rather stately progress round the estate, handsome, assured and still in very fine voice, even if the pitch is a trifle higher.

In addition to the phoney ferals, there are those who really can't decide whether they are wild or not. Our own beautiful girl, Evie, suffers several identity crises every day; when she is wild, she is very, very wild and when she feels like being a domestic pussycat she can put on a very convincing show.

We all have our funny little ways, but it would be helpful to have some indication of which Evie is in residence at different times of day. I remember a Time Management course I attended years ago where we were exhorted to display a red card if we could not be disturbed and a green card if callers were welcome. Or perhaps it was the other way round – and if I was confused by this relatively simple instruction, it's hardly surprising that Time Management and I never really hit it off.

Anyway, little black Evie – who looks like a real cat, unlike most of our other feline residents who tend to have bits missing – specialises in sudden, shrill screams should we make any attempt to handle her when her imaginary red card is on display. This usually follows a session of manic purring and jumping up on desks and chairs for headrubs and tickles. Lulled into thinking that Evie would welcome more attention half an hour later, we will blunder up to her – in our crashingly insensitive way – to be confronted by a diminutive panther that will have no option but to tear us limb from limb if we don't open the door *immediately*.

Evie combines this capriciousness with a rare gift for humour. Her favourite joke is the urgent, 'I must get outside now before I chuck up' one, which will always have us unseating any sleepy cat from our laps and probably the odd glass of El Plonko, in a stampede for the door. She will then look at us as if we've totally lost our marbles and skip on to the chair to slurp down half a plate of cat biscuits. The charm of this comedy is that Evie never tires of it and can keep it up for hours. I hardly need add that the one time we refuse to get up is inevitably the time she vomits profusely over the carpet, the patio door and , quite possibly, Benjamin Wobble, only pausing to fling a triumphant glare in the general direction of the sofa at the two pathetic humans who are putty in her paws.

Skippy

CHAPTER NINE

WILD WORDS

There's something about dealing with feral cats that makes us humans reacquaint ourselves with our wilder side, particularly in the language department. It is particularly unfortunate that many of our feral cat encounters have happened in close proximity to people who would shudder at the word 'puddings' should this be delivered in an overly robust manner.

One disgraceful incident occurred in the presence of an elderly lady when my friend and I had been called in to round up a feral cat and her kittens, who had obligingly located themselves in a garden shed. All we had to do was sidle in, gauntlets and cat carriers to the fore, grab the mother and scoop up the babies. It was not our choice that the old lady accompanied us, but we decided to smile through that little difficulty although it did mean things were on the cramped side of cosy in the cluttered shed.

We were terrified that we would inadvertently crush a tiny furry body amongst the precariously stacked wooden boxes and paint tins, but after a while the eerie stillness began to get to us and we started to move one or two obstacles. The removal of a box exposed an open window, which filled us with dismay. The eerie stillness could so easily be explained by the mother cat having removed the kittens before we got there. I was horrified by this possibility; my friend was furious.

'Well, f*** me rigid!' she ranted. 'You do realise that the cat and kittens could be anywhere now!'

The old lady shrugged, her ash-laded cigarette shedding generously down her stained housecoat.

My friend was outraged by this lack of contrition and launched into another expletive-riddled lecture, aided and abetted by me when I was able to get a word in. By now the cigarette was wobbling dangerously and it seemed likely that the whole shed would go up in smoke any minute. We were saved from further disgrace by the sudden appearance of a tiny black and white face peeping out from a pile of newspapers.

From that moment, we focussed our energies on finding the kittens and after a mere two hours of extremely careful rummaging we had gathered up four wriggling, squealing black and white babies. When we emerged from the shed, the last thing we expected to see was the kittens' mother rolling on the grass in what can only be described as a provocative manner. We set a trap and within seconds she had strolled in. Our ash-sprinkled friend coughed productively and smirked self-importantly, obviously feeling that she alone should be credited with the success of the operation. She generously agreed to have the mother cat back in due course if we would agree to provide cat food, but in the event the cat turned out to be nervy rather than feral and we were able to find a rather more reliable and loving home for her.

Another shed project followed closely on the heels of this and got off to an unfortunate start. The weather was on the warm side of tropical and I had been sweating it out in a cramped office all day. When I arrived home, not only were my own cats screaming abuse at me and rummaging for the RSPCA's emergency number, but the telephone was ringing in a way that made me dread picking up the receiver.

I was vaguely aware of the answerphone clicking on as I dolloped out an irresistible selection of Kittydins, but as I caught the words, 'missing kitten', I hurled myself at the receiver.

'Yes – we'd been seeing it around. Tiny it was – all mixed colours and pretty wild. I was scared it would bite the children, 'cos you can't expect kids to understand, can you? Anyway, I think it must have been living in the shed with its mother, but it's not there now and neither is its mother.'

A cold feeling came over me, in spite of the heat in the bungalow.

'How do you know it's not in the shed?' I asked. 'I suppose you've looked for it?'

There was an exaggerated sigh of exasperation. 'We know they're not there because the shed's not there. My husband took it down this morning.'

Silly me! I changed from my old work clothes into my even older cat rescue clothes and shoved the car in the general direction of the dismantled shed. I was greeted by more children than were good for me – or them – and waded through them as I tried to hear what the droopy woman in the doorway was saying. I never did really catch on, but at last succeeded in fighting my way through to the back garden where amongst the general wilderness of broken toys and bulging black bin bags I could make out the wooden floor of the flattened shed.

I am never at my best surrounded by small noisy rude children and the added ingredients of panic, tiredness and soaring temperatures did nothing to improve my temper. It must have been something I said, because within a commendably short time the dear little children had disappeared indoors and I was left alone to contemplate the lifeless crater that was the back garden of No 32.

It seemed like a good idea to have a rummage around the shed base and I donned my trusty gauntlets to probe the weeds and holes around the base. After a very short time, my hands were drenched in sweat and I couldn't have felt a writhing puma cub, never mind a tiny feral kitten. I ripped off the gloves and continued poking under the floorboards.

My! What strong little teeth that baby had! Even if I'd had the presence of mind to try to shake it off, that kitten was attached to my hand like an extra furry tortoiseshell finger. My language, gentle reader, was atrocious; in fact even the rabid kitten seemed shocked, but even as the blood dripped down my arm, I was overwhelmed with relief. There is nothing worse than worrying yourself sick about a lost and orphaned kitten at three in the morning.

I asked the over-enthusiastic shed demolishers to keep an eye out for the return of the mother cat, detached the kitten by gripping its scrawny scruff with my free hand and set off home. Once installed in a kitten pen, I could see that my erstwhile adversary was no more than a severely dehydrated, skinny baby in urgent need of liquid sustenance. She was far too young to be weaned and I hurriedly mixed up some kitten milk. She spat feebly, but the poor little soul was so exhausted by the heat and stress of her unimaginably dreadful day that I was able to hold her and get some nourishment down her parched throat.

I took her into the garden which was now pleasantly cool and walked round to the cat pens which housed several families. As I walked past one pen my tortie waif screamed. The resident nursing mother cat immediately hurled herself at the wire and stared at the tiny kitten. I went into the safety passage and held the kitten out, allowing the mother cat to sniff her. Within seconds the mother cat had grabbed the kitten by the scruff of the neck and disappeared back into the cat house, pausing only to shoot a contemptuous glance in my direction. Creeping out later to peep through the window, I could see a mound of white fur punctuated by five furry exclamation marks: four black and white and one tortoiseshell.

In due course we rounded up the kitten's mother and had her spayed. She was extremely wild and the people there – now the proud owners of a splendid new shed – were happy to feed her, so she was returned to them. The kitten – who we called 'Extra' – became fairly tame and was taken on by a kind couple who said they didn't expect miracles. This was lucky because little Extra had what we like to describe as a 'strong' personality, which manifested itself in some fairly challenging behaviour. I shall not go into detail, but the bathmat came in for a series of punishing boil washes.

After several difficult months, during which this sainted couple were severely tested, I was dreading a phone call telling me they couldn't cope with her any longer. I didn't have a clue what I would do with Extra if this happened because by now she wouldn't be wild enough to live safely in feral conditions and I couldn't imagine who would take her on if she hadn't made go of things with these lovely people. Spookily, the call came just as I was chewing the problem over for the umpteenth time.

'It's Graham here. I'm so sorry to disturb you, but I wanted to tell you about Extra.'

'Yes – I've been expecting you to ring. I realise how patient you've been with her and how difficult things have been...'

'I suppose they have really. It was such a shock last night when Sue had dropped off to sleep on the sofa and I realised the cat was cuddled up on her lap. I reached out and stroked Extra and she...'

'She what?' I squeaked. 'She didn't bite you, did she?'

Graham chuckled. 'No, nothing like that! She purred her little heart out!'

So overwhelmed was I by this news that I very nearly swore.

CHAPTER TEN

The Famous Five

The 'Famous Five' first came to our attention by means of a panicky phone call from office workers employed on an industrial estate on the outskirts of Woking. There was a mother cat and four large kittens and they were all ginger. A friend and I went to assess the situation and I can't begin to tell you how thrilled we were to discover that the 'large kittens' were in fact only marginally smaller than their mother, so any hopes we may have treasured of taming them and finding them homes disappeared with the speed of a cat when a vet visit looms.

For the twitch of a cat's tail we deluded ourselves that prolonged contact with the girls who fed them might have taught them some manners, but the sight of them with backs arched and ears back as we walked into their territory soon brought us to our senses.

In our heads we were berating these lovely ladies for not contacting us sooner; what we actually said was how well they had done feeding them and providing shelter because they all looked wonderful. We expressed surprise that there hadn't been any other litters between the birth of the famous five and our arrival and were told that the tom cat who fathered the kittens had moved away. Thank goodness for small mercies!

Obviously it wouldn't be long before the babies were mature enough to begin the demanding task of expanding the

Ginger Dynasty, so we pulled ourselves together and arranged to return with traps.

'Please don't feed them before we come,' we asked. 'They'll be suspicious of the traps and we want them good and hungry or they won't go in.'

On the appointed morning we clanked into the yard with three steel traps and enough bait to trap a pride of lions.

'They haven't been fed, have they?' I asked, just by way of conversation.

'Well… When I got here this morning I felt so sorry for the poor little mites that I did give them some warm milk; and then they were still looking a bit sad so I just gave them a few biscuits. But they haven't had much because I remembered you said not to feed them.'

So what part of not feeding them didn't you understand, I wanted to scream, but didn't – mainly because I'd just cut my finger on a sharp edge and was fully occupied trying to stem the flow.

In due course, all three traps were baited and with some effort we had succeeded in persuading the workers to go indoors. Apart from wanting to get them away from the cats, we were quite keen on them making some coffee for us.

Just as we were warming our hands round the steaming mugs, however, Iris wandered over to the window.

'Oh, the poor things!' she exclaimed. 'There's a cat in each of the traps! They must be soooo frightened!'

This was no time for misplaced wobbliness and we reluctantly abandoned our coffee to rush outside, fling covers over the traps and load them into the car. We had to take the trapped cats back to the pen in the garden to decant them in order to free up two traps to catch the remaining 'baby' and its mother.

Soon we were back to commence Phase Two and were feeling smug beyond belief when Mumpuss sidled into the trap. Just one kitten to go, then it would be coffee time.

We once again withdrew into the offices and watched as the remaining youngster skirted round the trap. An hour later, we were still watching him.

'It's funny he's being so difficult,' said one of the girls suddenly. 'Because he's the friendliest of them and often comes into the office.'

The words bounced round my head.

'He comes in?' I asked incredulously. 'If he comes in and we can shut the door, we can catch him by hand. Can you lure him in with food? Is there a separate room?'

As I spoke I was looking round at the open plan office space which covered an area the equivalent of two aircraft hangars.

'There's the kitchen,' responded a helpful voice. 'We might be able to get him in there.'

Five minutes and a plate of minced chicken later, there was a resounding slam and the cat was shut in the kitchen. All I had to do was slide in and grab him. Hardly a challenge!

Getting into the kitchen was much easier than I'd expected because it was absolutely enormous. I saw the cat at the far end and we staged a bizarre re-enactment of *High Noon,* stalking towards each other until the cat's nerve gave out and he took avoiding action behind a very large fridge.

I wrenched the fridge forward, tipping it in the process, and a stream of expletives somehow left my mouth as a container of milk spilt over me. My quarry shot off and managed to squeeze into a large cupboard under the sink.

As I crawled around in the darkness grabbing at shadows, I could hear my friend chatting animatedly on the other side of the door.

'Gotcha, you little bugger!' I screamed as I scruffed an extremely startled pack of dishcloths.

Eventually, when both the poor cat and I were exhausted and my companion had pretty well lost her voice in a doomed attempt to drown the worst of my language, I managed to scruff him and didn't even have the strength to swear when he piddled down my leg.

It wasn't possible for these beautiful cats to return to the industrial estate as they were not universally welcome and, although the office workers were more than happy to continue feeding them, it was a dangerous place in more ways than one. Fork lift trucks and a whole army of vehicles were constantly shunting about like an intricate country dance involving prehistoric monsters and there were numerous opportunities for adventurous cats to be incarcerated or squashed.

We therefore had to find them another home to go to once they had been neutered and spayed and realised that there was very little chance of finding somewhere where they could stay together. In a remarkably short space of time we had interest from a very sensible woman running an equestrian centre, who wanted a couple of cats to keep the rodent population in check. After another couple of conversations she had agreed to take three, on the basis that their mother would be devastated to be parted from so many of her babies; when after a further chat she thought that four would be manageable, we were pretty well home and dry and in due course a friend and I took all five cats to their new home.

It was a relief to arrive and find that everything was ready for the new arrivals, but not quite such good news to learn that the cats and their temporary shelters had to be carried over a large muddy field to a distant barn. Still, nothing like a bracing walk in howling wind and lashing rain with cat carriers crashing into the backs of your legs to put the roses back in your cheeks – or, in my case, to make your nose glow like Rudolph's and your varifocals freeze to your face.

Once the large metal pens had been erected, all we had to do was decant the cats from the cages into the pens. This was accomplished with only minimal drama and recriminations –

and, as usual, it was the humans who behaved badly; the cats remained calm and rational throughout.

The Famous Five have been there for years now, in the most idyllic setting imaginable, catching mice when they can be bothered to, which really isn't all that often. Over the years they have mellowed and now take a polite interest in riding lessons, although so far they've not taken to the saddle themselves. I wouldn't rule it out though; Charlotte Dujardin needs to keep a tight grip on the reins!

CHAPTER ELEVEN

Mothers of Courage

Pansy

Over the years I've met many courageous cats – cats who would put a few humans that I've encountered to shame.

Nowhere has feline bravery been more in evidence than with mother cats who have been prepared to risk their lives to save their kittens. If only we could have persuaded them that we were on their side and that their babies would be safe with us! I always found it slightly hurtful to think that these poor cats thought their kittens would be safer living behind dustbins or on railway embankments where foxes and rats abounded than they would be in the care of Cats Protection workers, but I suppose I would feel the same way if a Martian tried to snatch one of my cats away.

Not only are mother cats amazingly brave; they are also fantastically clever and none more so than Helen.

I could tell from his voice that the man who phoned me had had an unnerving experience. He lived in a flat above the shops in the High Street, Weybridge and had been away on a training course for a few days. As usual he had left the bathroom window slightly open and when he returned had been surprised, to put it mildly, to find the wardrobe door open and a collection of jumpers and shoes strewn across the bedroom floor. There was no sign of anything having been stolen, so he suspected that an erstwhile girlfriend, who had held on to a key, might have popped in.

Having convinced himself that this must have been the explanation, he suffered a further shock when he went to put his clothes away in the wardrobe and was met with a barrage of spits and growls. Amongst an impressive clutter of socks, shoes and shirts crouched a small white and tabby cat, shielding a litter of tiny, mouse-like kittens with her emaciated body.

I can only say in my defence that I really wasn't very well when I took that phone call because I left without my stock-in-trade gauntlets – an omission that I became painfully aware of when I bent down to speak to Mumpuss. To say that she wasn't impressed with my attempts to coax her out of the wardrobe would be an understatement; she indicated a strong desire to kill me or, at the very least, redesign my face. In this re-run of *The Lion, the Witch and the Wardrobe* she had obviously decided I was the witch.

I asked if I could borrow some gloves and was presented with some oven gloves that might as well have been carved in oak. These gloves had seen some serious action and from the grease that adhered to their singed surfaces, I would wager that salads were not a significant part of my new friend's diet. Not that it was up to me to make judgements, but catching hold of a wild cat is pretty tricky at the best of times and trying to do so with stiff greasy gloves certainly adds a further note of challenge.

Eventually, I managed to ease the mother cat out of the wardrobe and shut the door as well as I could while she circled the bedroom at head height. Meanwhile the young man made helpful comments, such as, 'Mind she doesn't scratch you!'

In the end, it was a combination of sheer exhaustion and luck – as it so often is in life – which achieved the desired result and the little cat was banged up in the carrier. Removing the kittens from the wardrobe was a doddle after the earlier circuit training round the bed and soon they were snuggling down in a separate carrier – separate in case Mumpuss should inadvertently trample them on the journey to the cat pen.

The mess in the wardrobe had to be seen to be believed – but preferably not on a full stomach. I pulled out a congealed selection of soiled socks, shirts and what might have been sportswear and asked if there was a plastic sack I could dump the lot in.

'Yes – I suppose that would be an idea. I think the laundry basket's full and it might be a few days before I get round to rinsing them through.'

Rinsing them through? Those clothes needed soaking in bleach, boiling for days and then burying in a plague pit half-a-mile deep.

We decided that the cat should be called 'Helen', after the ex-girlfriend who was initially suspected of popping in and dragging out the soiled contents of his wardrobe. I'm sure she would have been overwhelmed.

As a little aside, I have occasionally been burbling away about my adventures with feral cats when I have become aware of increasing nervousness on the part of my companions. I have now realised that this nervousness often coincides with episodes involving solitary men, wild cats and bedrooms. Some people lead such sheltered lives!

Even I was slightly concerned when I had a call to go to a man's house one evening to help him catch a visiting wild cat. He was perfectly happy to keep the cat but quite rightly thought it should be checked over and neutered. I was on my own at the time and took the precaution of telling my next door neighbour where I was going and when I expected to return. She was extremely concerned about the wisdom of this enterprise, but I couldn't help noticing that her concern didn't quite extend to coming with me!

I arrived with gauntlets and cat carrier and adopted what I hoped was a professional, no-nonsense manner. We squeezed into a small and rather untidy bedroom and in no time at all had the cat pinned in a corner. I was closing in to scruff the terrified creature when it leapt up the man's leg and latched on to a particularly vulnerable part of his anatomy with its back legs dangling. I hate to see a man cry, but suffice it to say that everybody knew each other a whole lot better by the time the cat had been hauled off him and shoved into the carrier.

I digress. Although she fought like a demon to defend her kittens, Helen in due course reached a stage where the attractions of being pummelled and sucked at began to wane and by the time we needed to handle the babies in order to socialise them she really was much more interested in getting her fur done and having a bit of fun. Our robust approach to spaying may have limited the potential for fun, but Helen turned out to be rather a sweet cat and found a caring home. Her babies, needless to say, pretty well homed themselves; I suspect their new owners were still calling them the Wardrobe Kittens and dining out on their early adventures when they and the kittens were drawing their pensions.

How my heart leapt when I was told about a cat and five kittens that had been discovered living in a disused private car park in the centre of Woking! My excitement increased to dangerous levels when I learned that the car park was locked and had to be accessed by means of keying in a secret number and hoping for the best. Another winning feature was that the natives – apart from one wonderful couple who were extremely worried about the cats – were anything but supportive. The only possible food source before this couple discovered the family was an international buffet of takeaway remains laced, I suspect, with a number of interesting condiments.

It is always difficult to know what to do in such situations. There is only one certainty, and that is that the kittens and mother cat will never enter the traps in the desired order. There is the worrying knowledge that if a cat is trapped once and released prematurely – i.e. before being spayed or whatever – the chances of catching it again are somewhere minus zilch and so on this particular occasion when the mother cat went into the trap and triggered it, I reluctantly set off with her to the vet's, leaving her kittens to fend for themselves in the car park.

A further complication was that I knew the location was about as inhospitable as it could possibly be and from the start had it in mind to relocate the mother cat and hopefully find homes for the kittens. This ruled out the possibility of returning the mother to her babies and there was therefore an overwhelming need to round up the kittens sooner rather than later. I cannot speak highly enough here of the efforts made by my great friend, Karen. And for those readers who have bravely fought their way through my earlier books, this is indeed the same wonderful Karen who comes to look after the current residents of Tresta Towers. (We tell her we're going on holiday, but it's actually for rehabilitation and assessment.)

An interesting aspect of this trapping project was that

three of the kittens did a disappearing act. Karen succeeded in trapping the others, having realised that they were too light to trigger the trap mechanism and taken the appropriate steps to remedy the problem. We feared the worst about the missing kittens, who – just as we had almost given up hope – miraculously reappeared looking none the worse for whatever adventure they had enjoyed.

Their mother was an extremely feisty young lady who must have been a pet at one time, since she had been seen wearing a bedraggled and very tight blue collar. As I staggered down the steep slope from the car park to the vet's, she shoved a slim, piebald leg through the bars of the trap and ripped the back of my leg – through some fairly tough old jeans, I should add. Thank heavens I wasn't wearing a frothy little Laura Ashley frock! She needed a name, of course, for reference purposes and I christened her Pansy, just because it seemed so inappropriate for such a spirited little minx.

Pansy's joy when her babies were restored to her in the cat pen was touching, to say the least. What wasn't quite so touching was her tendency to rip me apart every time I went into the pen and tried to get close to the kittens. It was painfully obvious that any human handling of her babies was not on Pansy's agenda. Equally obvious was the fact that the kittens were now about ten weeks old and if we were to stand any chance of finding homes for them, they would have to have some concentrated handling in the very near future.

Efforts to find somewhere for Pansy to go failed miserably and so I decided she would have to stay with me, living wild if that was what she chose to do or becoming a pet if she felt like it. You could be forgiven for thinking that faced with the prospect of freedom any self-respecting, self-styled feral would bolt for the far horizon. Not only did Pansy take no interest in the open door – she rushed inside the cat house to take up her position in front of the kittens that I was obviously intending to dismember. It was a hot day and I was melting in a deeply unattractive way, while Pansy stamped and spat at me every time I approached the door of the house.

After an hour or so, I had succeeded in getting her into the safety passage of the pen and was about to fling open the outer door when I realised one of the kittens was with her. There followed another desperate half hour of shepherding and nudging to get the kitten back in without Pansy darting back into the pen with it. Finally, the kittens were locked up in the pen and Pansy was in the safety passage with the outer door open and I crawled indoors to pour myself an extremely large glass of El Plonko, confident that Pansy would have disappeared into the night when I went back outside.

Fortunately, anybody who works with cats is used to being wrong, so returning under cover of darkness to find Pansy still in the safety passage wasn't too much of a self-esteem crisis for me. She had moved into the garden by the early morning, but wouldn't stray far from the babies, always keeping them in view and becoming visibly concerned when I went in with them.

Our dear ginger brain-damaged boy, Benjamin Wobble, was in heaven. Always thrilled to see kittens in the pens, he spent hours with Pansy in happy contemplation of what I'm sure he thought of as their little family and, probably sensing that he was no threat to her or to the babies, Pansy was happy to have him there. Meanwhile I and an army of wonderful volunteers were trying to make up for lost time and handling the kittens as much as possible. We never expected gratitude, but the spitting and shrill growling that greeted our efforts was a little unfair as this was their only hope of achieving homes.

We decided they should all be given names beginning with 'V', so we had Volvo, Vernon, Victor, Vladimir and Velma – there being only one girl. They grew amazingly quickly and we realised we were fighting against the clock in terms of taming them as they may well have been older than our original estimate. Everybody needs a bit of luck every now and then, however, and we were certainly lucky in finding understanding people who were prepared to give these spiky teenagers a home. As a precaution, we had them all neutered and spayed before they were homed, just to be on the safe side.

It was sad to see Pansy lurking round the pen once her kittens had gone to begin their new lives, but it had to be done and meanwhile she had Benjamin Wobble to console her.

CHAPTER TWELVE

Psycho Sadie – More Front than Selfridges

A common belief – amongst non-cat people – is that a cat is just a cat. The internet has, of course, done much to erode this view as cats have taken to YouTube with aplomb, obviously wondering why they had to wait so long to seize the cyber stage. Still, however, the view persists that any cat choosing to walk alone, or at any rate to eschew total dependency on the human race, must be 'just a cat'.

In the course of this book I hope I have shown that feral cats have distinct personalities and could not be accused of lacking character. In fact, many have more character than might be considered an asset, exerting a formidable influence over their beleaguered humans.

One such cat is Psycho Sadie, a very small tortoiseshell feral, who I only met recently, although I had had the pleasure of sighting her in her leafy retreat a couple of years previously. The fact that I only recently saw Sadie at close quarters has in no way prevented me from appreciating what a power pack she is, due to receiving regular accounts of her exploits from a close friend – a friend who is inclined towards understatement rather than exaggeration, I should add.

One thing that many cats are good at harbouring is grudges. This can be against a person, all men, all carrier bags, M&S carrier bags, the Rolling Stones or the world in general. Logic occasionally comes into it, but the grudges that cats are most fond of frequently have no basis in fact. Even if there is a reason for holding the grudge in the first place, cats have a tendency to become fonder of them over time. They are also adept at appearing to have got over a grudge, only to wheel it out again at a later date – usually just as you're telling somebody how they used to bite children, but fortunately haven't done it for years. At that moment, little Darren will lurch through the door with blood dripping from his finger, pursued by Cuddles.

Little Sadie undeniably had a very bad start in life, but that is a very long time ago and her luck changed almost immediately. None of this has influenced Sadie's jaundiced view of the human race.

Nobody could claim that being a tiny helpless kitten alone in a rabbit burrow was a happy situation, but against the odds a passing gamekeeper heard her piping cries, reached into the burrow and extracted a spitting clawing creature the size of a mouse. Praise is due here because many people would have stuffed her straight back down the rabbit hole, but gamekeepers are probably more used to ungrateful animals than most people are and he presented her to a friend who had mentioned that she might think about having a kitten.

There is, of course, a slight difference between thinking about having a kitten and having a squawking ball of fluff deposited in one's lap, but Sadie's luck held and she now had a home.

Although she had landed herself the cushiest billet imaginable, Sadie kept faith with her wild beginnings. She spent most of her time outside, allocating only brief spells for socialising with her besotted human, while condescending to consume an array of expensive cat food more commonly sighted at the more upmarket type of cat show. Sadie didn't believe in making life easy for her owner, possibly subscribing to the theory that playing hard to get would enhance her appeal and also in some strange way induce feelings of guilt in this vulnerable human.

The 'playing hard to get' behaviour inevitably peaked when a visit to the vet was necessary. As the years went by, Sadie became less robust and arthritis took its toll, so that the ensuing contest between a fit and active woman and a tiny frail cat was obviously not a fair one. So quite why Sadie always won paws down is one of life's freakier mysteries.

Sadie moved to Scotland a couple of years ago, to a large house in wild and idyllic surroundings. Sadie's owner recognised that Sadie's reduced mobility would make it impossible for her to climb the stairs to the cosiest rooms and therefore decided to choose a downstairs room so that Sadie could join her when she felt inclined. It took Sadie a couple of days to realise that things were pretty damn cosy on the first floor and she was just a tortoiseshell blur as she climbed the stairs on her rickety little legs.

In years past, Sadie has revelled in a good scrap, but recently had a run-in with the local bully boy that laid her low. Unable to stand, things looked bleak. At sixteen years and riddled with arthritis, it looked as if this plucky fighter had reached the end of the road. Her owner was devastated and knew only too well what needed to be done. Needless to say, Sadie had no intention of making things easy and had to be scruffed for the dreaded vet trip to the vet's, screaming abuse throughout the journey and the examination – abuse which rose to a glass-shattering crescendo when the vet's probing located a deep wound on her back leg.

The vet was slightly surprised when Sadie's owner burst into tears and thought that the old feral must have managed to injure her during the battle on the surgery table.

'Do you think she might get over it?' the poor woman gasped between sobs. 'I thought she'd broken her pelvis or shattered her leg…'

'Get over it? I'm rather afraid she will!' snorted the vet, shoving a syringe full of antibiotics into Psycho Sadie skinny neck and ramming her back in the carrier.

God bless the feisty old cat, I say. And God bless her owner, who loves her beyond reason – an over-rated commodity in my humble opinion.

CHAPTER THIRTEEN

The Later Years

Spitfire

We don't have as many cats now, although what I consider to be a perfectly normal number still raises eyebrows.

I recently popped into the nearest supermarket to top up our dwindling supply of cat food as the bulk order had been delayed and the check out lady surveyed the pile of pouches and tins with amazement.

'My goodness!' she chirped, 'however many cats have you got?'

I could, of course, just have suggested it was none of her business, but she was a cheery soul and that would have seemed unnecessarily harsh.

'We're down to nine now,' I said. 'It seems strange not to have so many.'

She shook her head slightly, smiled in a kindly manner and no doubt stored this little cameo away to have a good old chortle over in her coffee break.

Obviously, a giving a home to a relatively large number of cats only works if there is room for everybody to have their own space. Age and character also come into the equation and most of our residents are elderly with a generous sprinkling of special needs.

We had to say farewell to our dear ginger boy, Benjamin Wobble, at nine years of age, which was a huge sadness to Roger and me and to the many friends who loved this fuzzy teddy bear. Benjy had significant neurological problems having succumbed to toxoplasmosis as a tiny kitten, but enjoyed more cuddles than most teddy bears could ever dream of having. There are many jumpers and sweatshirts in cupboards across the land that haven't quite recovered from Benjy's ecstatic and dribbling embrace.

At the time of writing we have six and a half domestic cats and two and a half ferals. The halves come together in our beautiful black girl, Evie, who as I explained previously has feral times and non-feral times and this would be fine if only we could recognise at an earlier stage how things stood.

Count Lucio, who is sixteen and a martyr to recurring episodes of pancreatitis, is still more handsome than any large black moggy has a right to be and spends most nights on my pillow, draped fetchingly round my head. What can be quite a cosy thing in the depths of winter is slightly less welcome in a heatwave, but I wouldn't hurt his feelings for the world.

And then there is Whizzy, our wonderful white and black

three-legged girl who found it so hard to settle with us five years ago and is now a much-loved matriarch – loved by her humans, that is; I think her fellow felines might take a different view. Whizzy's particular party trick is heaving herself up from floor to sofa by means of the nearest available leg. If that leg is not encased in steel and the owner of it happens to let out a shriek of surprise or, quite possibly, agony, Whizzy will glare at him or her and dig in all the more. She really is a sweet creature and once she is settled on a lap one could not wish for a more restful companion. She particularly enjoys a good right ear rub – as she is missing her right hind leg – before we all nod off in front of the television.

Tiny Trixie-Tribble, our Pets as Therapy star, has been with us for four years now and is not quite such a heat-seeking missile as she was when she arrived. Her book, *From Sidcup with Purrs*, gives her version of her story, but suffice it to say she is quite unlike any other cat that we have ever had. Recently we discovered that she may be a 'toyger' – a cross between a pedigree Bengal and a domestic shorthair and the name certainly suits this mischievous, bouncy little tabby girl.

Harriet, who arrived as Smudge, but was so obviously a Harriet that we were compelled to recognise this at an early stage, came to us two years ago because she was unable to settle happily with two dogs after her elderly owner had died. She is eighteen now with the beginnings of kidney problems, but is as sprightly as a kitten and enjoys going in and out to the garden as frequently as possible and particularly when her humans are settling down on the sofa. She makes her requirements known by animated scratching on the patio door, her little white paws beating an insistent and extremely irritating rhythm on the glass, whether she is inside or out. Harriet is blessed with a rather sour expression which only lightens into the suggestion of a smile when one of the other cats suffers a misfortune, such as misjudging the height of the scratching post.

Stumpy Malone, author of *Paws for Thought*, is a sweet black boy who was born without back paws. If anybody ever thought that this would in any way restrict Stumpy's lifestyle, they were mistaken. Stumpy is six years old now and his disability gave us the excuse we needed to adopt a kitten. He is a relentlessly cheerful little cat and climbs trees, often hanging from his front paws while twisting his body round to grab the branch with his back legs. A rather serious locum vet was reduced to an emotional wreck when Stumpy was presented for his annual booster jabs and described him as 'an inspiration', rushing for her phone to photograph him. Our hero was unfazed by this attention, being very much more interested in the stethoscope that dangled so tantalisingly inches from his nose.

Stumpy Malone has recently taken an interest in the glamorous Persian who has moved into the bungalow next door. I fear that it is a doomed passion, as the Lady Cussie appears to be quite oblivious to Stumpy's charms, either gazing into space or turning her back in a rather hurtful manner. Looking at the Persian's impressive pedigree, I derived some innocent amusement from imagining 'Stumpy Malone' featuring alongside more impressive titles such as 'Grand Champion Seaspray Conundrum' or 'Whipped Cream Whispering Choux Bun'. Alas, for a number of reasons – all of them good ones – this is unlikely to be a concern for the Governing Council of the Cat Fancy.

Our latest arrival is the Lady Mollypops, a sweet grey girl who is fourteen years old, but getting younger. She seemed quite a serious little cat when she joined us, but over the months we have seen her become increasingly playful and cheeky. This has given us great joy, even if she has become rather bossy in the kitchen, having strong views about how long the chicken should roast for and even stronger views on who should have it.

And then there are our two feral girls, Pansy and Spitfire.

Pansy has, I suspect and hope, forgotten all about her kittens that she raised under such challenging circumstances after eight or so years of easier living. She now lives at the front of the bungalow, but is a cat of many lives and more than one address. She doesn't look any older than the day when she so affectionately raked her claws down my leg as I lurched towards the door of the veterinary surgery, but her contours are distinctly more rounded and she has a knowing rather than a hungry look.

We don't know where she disappears to at night, but she is almost always waiting at the kitchen door for breakfast and more often than not has a friend with her. Pansy is an incorrigible flirt and likes to have a boyfriend or two on the go at all times. Her current squeeze is Silver Collar (not his real name as we don't want to cause discord if he is in a relationship) and this slightly challenged black boy is obviously besotted with heartless little Pansy, who I fear will ditch him if something younger and sportier should make an appearance.

Pansy is well known to our cat-loving neighbours who love her piebald prettiness and skittish ways. We often see her white paws twinkling along in the darkness when we drive home after a meeting or get-together with friends. She frequently comes from some way down our little cul-de-sac, knowing the sound of our car engine and knowing also that a plate of food will appear as soon as we arrive home.

Pansy must be about ten years old now and although she will rub round our legs we cannot touch her. We haven't made significant efforts to tame her, because she has chosen to live outside and I firmly believe that cats are safer in these circumstances if they retain their wildness. Much as I love foxes, I do not trust them if they are desperately hungry and have cubs to feed; they are predators and will do what they need to do to survive. I don't blame them, of course, but neither do I believe that we should put at risk the animals for which we have assumed responsibility.

So there is Pansy, frisking and frolicking in the front garden, while our senior wild girl, Spitfire, resides in the back garden. Spitfire is seventeen now, and her once jet-black fur is a rustier shade of darkness. She was extraordinarily close to our glamorous long-haired tortoiseshell, Delilah, for many years and after Delilah died allowed herself a brief period of mourning before seeming to pull herself together and get on with her life. Her mourning took the form of wandering round the garden wailing for her friend, but even as she did so she seemed to know that she had gone and would shake her head in a world-weary way.

Spitfire is almost totally deaf now and her poor old joints are stiffening up after so many years of outside living. At the beginning of last winter we fretted about her capacity for surviving not just the inevitable cold, but the dampness that gets into old bones. There are several cat chalets still in Kitty City – an area of the garden that we have always regarded as Wild Cat Haven – but even with frequent changes of blankets and igloo beds it was impossible to keep them dry and warm without any source of power.

As some readers will know, when we first acquired Tiny Trixie-Tribble we realised that it would never be safe for her to roam freely because of her deafness and her total lack of fear, which would have seen her flinging herself at any passing and possibly cat-eating Rottweiler. We decided to buy a cattery-style cat pen where on sunny days Miss Tiny could take the air in safety. Unfortunately, we failed to discuss the matter with Tiny, who the moment she was placed in the pen screamed her head off and continued to do so for half-an-hour, by which time we had pretty well lost the will to live.

It was obvious that this had not been one of our better ideas as Tiny saw herself not as a cat, but as a person who could perfectly well sit on a patio lounger or inspect the flower beds accompanied by her doting servants; why would such a superior being need to be banged up in a cage like some ordinary sort of cat?

The pen was used sporadically to house other cats, but generally stood empty and reproachfully on the patio, waiting patiently to come into its own as Spitfire's bijou winter residence.

With heated beds installed and every crack and crevice draft-proofed, it only remained for Poor Roger to cut a cat-flap sized hole in the outer door and with the inner pen door propped open all was in readiness. There were four beds to choose from on two floors, well above the ground, and Spitfire took to it like a chilly feral to a cosy penthouse suite.

We were delighted. No longer would we lie awake at night worrying about her getting cold, or being attacked by marauding foxes; instead we could drift off to sleep secure in the knowledge that if she wasn't exactly dreaming the dreams of the innocent, she was at least safe and warm.

Unfortunately, this cosy vision was shattered when after a few nights we found her huddled on the patio and a trail of large muddy pawprints covering the floor of the pen. Her food bowls had been overturned and there wasn't a morsel to be seen. We tried to kid ourselves it was a hedgehog, but we knew she wouldn't have been so frightened of Mrs Prickles – although the size of the pawprints made even a hedgehog seem a pretty scary prospect if it needed feet that big. Poor Roger was on the case immediately. A bush cam was purchased and rigged up in the garden so that we would soon know who the culprit was.

Trust me, gentle and patient reader, you would not have believed it. The beast that had squeezed through the tiny, cat-sized aperture was none other than dear old badger! How such a porky creature had managed it defies belief, but the camera does not lie and within a heartbeat Poor Roger remedied the situation by making the hole smaller.

Noting this modification with obvious satisfaction, Spitfire moved back in and once again all was sweetness and light at Tresta Towers.

So there we are with just two wild cats now, where once there were many, but some concessions have to be made to the passing of the years and it is important to recognise when the time has come to scale down one's activities so as not to become a pain in the backside to others. Our niche in the market nowadays is very much to provide a safe haven for the old and disabled domestic cats who need and deserve a caring and quiet home in which to dribble the days away.

I shall always have a soft spot for the ferals – those wonderful spirited cats who have survived abandonment, persecution and every crime that can and is visited upon innocent animals by callous, selfish humans.

And to finish on a lighter note: a wild cat in your garden makes a far more interesting conversation piece than a mass-produced and garish gnome. It's also far less likely to be stolen by drunken revellers or suffer from flaky paint syndrome.

Spitfire in her Cabin

APPENDIX ONE

Feral Facts

The major cat charities are united in their view that there are more cats and kittens than there are good homes available – in the UK as well as other parts of the world that we like to think of as less enlightened (there isn't too much justification for this view, but it's the one we've grown fond of).

It therefore follows that neutering and spaying is necessary – not just with feral cats, but particularly so with them as most are likely to live their lives fending for themselves and the fewer kittens they produce the less misery there will be.

There is much to be said for blood testing ferals for the ghastly and terminal diseases, Feline Leukaemia and Feline 'Aids'. Both diseases can infect other cats and unfortunately feral colonies are particularly at risk as they live in close proximity to each other, are often un-neutered and in poor condition. It is clearly irresponsible to release infected animals if blood testing indicates they are suffering from one of these horrible diseases; it is also unfair to keep an animal which is essentially a free spirit in a cage for the rest of its life, so there can only be one answer.

This next point is rather a case of 'do as I say' rather than 'do what I always wanted to do', because I always found ear-tipping upsetting, although I'm sure it didn't matter to the cats and no doubt saved many needless operations by identifying those cats that had already been 'adjusted'. The standard, internationally recognised, sign that a cat has been neutered or spayed is the removal of the left ear tip so that it is clear that this has been done surgically rather than incurred in a fight. The vet will do this at the same time as performing the neutering operation, so the cat will know nothing about it.

Adult ferals will usually prove almost impossible to tame. To avoid prolonged and stressful incarceration, these cats should generally be blood-tested, neutered and returned to their original location. If they must be relocated, it's important to make sure that the new 'owner' realises they will need to be kept in a large cage or secure outhouse for approximately three weeks to enable them to bond with their new territory. Although they are wild, there needs to be an understanding that food, water and shelter will be provided. It is also helpful to leave a contact number with the person assuming responsibility for the cats in case of problems, including injury or illness. In such cases, it is likely that the cat will need to be trapped by people with the appropriate experience and equipment.

APPENDIX TWO

Taming Feral Kittens

The younger the kitten, the better the chances of taming it. Sometimes, this means that the kittens will come into the care of a charity before they are fully weaned. In certain circumstances the risk of a feral mother moving a litter away outweighs the merits of the kittens spending the optimum amount of time with her. If the kittens are young enough to require hand-rearing, they will associate handling with feeling full and contented and the taming is likely to happen without a paw being raised in anger.

The window of opportunity for making progress with kittens is a small one and every day counts. Most kittens will not come into care until they are around eight weeks old and are highly mobile, not to mention pretty feisty.

To avoid pursuing the kittens round a room, with the inevitable challenges of the kittens disappearing under sideboards or down the back of a wall unit, it makes sense to contain them in a cage or kitten pen. This means it will be easier to get hold of each kitten for handling sessions.

In my experience – and that's all I'm basing this advice on – frequent interactions for short periods of time work best. Before even attempting to scruff the kitten, it is often a good plan to introduce play in the form of fishing rod toys which can be twitched invitingly inside or outside the pen. While the diminutive Fluffy is playing, he will forget how frightened he is and how much he hates you.

Scruffing the kitten really is the best way of getting hold of it. It's what mother cats do and the kitten will be calmed by this contact. At first, just holding the kitten on your lap for a minute or so before returning it to its pen is a good strategy, repeating the exercise several times a day and building up the time that the kitten spends with you. Stroking with inanimate things like a soft brush or a toy rather than too much actual touching by hand also works well.

Once you have reached the stage where the kitten is confident enough to come out into the room without diving into an inaccessible bolt hole, rewards and play work well, together with frequent picking up and stroking.

Try not to be disappointed if progress is erratic; I have often gone to bed feeling that I've made a giant leap forward with Fluffy, only to find that in the morning he is looking at me as if he's never seen me before. Progress should be measured over a week or so rather than from day to day.

There will always be kittens that do not respond to our well-meaning efforts to tame them. My own dear old Spitfire is a case in point and my theory is that she and others like her come from a long line of ferals, so that their wildness is wired in. They also have not had the benefit of a domestic or semi-domesticated mother and may have come from remote locations where humans were rarely sighted.

However successful you are with taming such kittens, they are unlikely to ever be as bombproof as kittens that have been born in a home to a completely domesticated mother. Such kittens are likely to have been handled at a very early stage and as long as this has been the right sort of handling they are likely to respond positively.

It follows that a quieter home with adults is likely to be the happiest environment for Fluffy, or a home with older children who can understand that Fluffy is a very special cat indeed.

People sometimes express surprise that adult feral cats are not always attacking and brawling with their domestic cousins. The fact that they don't trust – and may actively dislike – humans doesn't mean that they don't get on with other cats, particularly when they've all been 'adjusted'. In fact, because they are generally used to living in colonies, feral cats are usually quite at ease with other felines, feral or domestic.